Lines

By Mark Neary

This book is dedicated to four men whom I didn't know at all a couple of years ago, but who have taught me so much about love, belief and balls.

Thank you: James Neary, William Culley, Tom Fleetwood and Charlie Worley

Acknowledgements.

Thank you to Kate, my self-appointed copy editor. If you ever find yourself all at sea in Brentford, or looking for a naval joke with suitable double-entendre, Kate is your woman.

Thanks to Val who listened with great vigour and kindness for hours as I gushed, "You never guess who I found living in Lea Road!"

And from the family, thanks to Jayne and Carol, who put up with endless phone calls, along the lines of: "What was the name of the shop in King Street where Mum used to buy her undies?"

Index:

The Neary/Worley Family

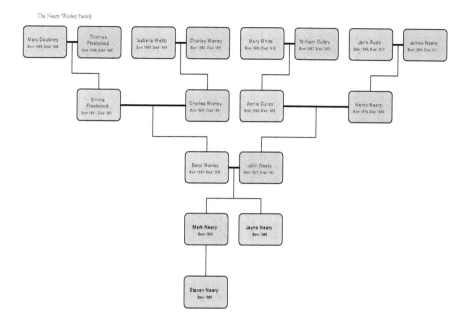

1. Prologue

Let's start with a dream from 2013.

I asked for the dream. I like asking for dreams that shed some light on a problem that I have been wrestling with. This dream sowed the seed for a six year long adventure.

In the dream, I was standing outside Gare Du Nord in Paris. Dozens of Parisians were enjoying an afternoon of wine and desserts in the July sunshine. At one table sat Peter Ustinov. He was immersed in a book and nobody appeared to be paying him any attention. Eventually, he took his leave and I noticed that he had left a small box behind on his table. As he walked away, he turned back and gestured towards me to take the box. He boarded a train and that was his last appearance in the dream. I sat down at the table that he had vacated and gingerly opened the box. The contents were: A spiral notebook with a heart on the cover; a copy of Viktor Frankl's 'Man's Search for Meaning'; a ballpoint pen and two balls – a golf ball and a tennis ball.

I woke up and knew that the dream would be called "Love, Belief & Balls."

It was shortly after the court case that Steven and I had been involved in and I had been giving lots of press and media interviews and telling our tale at conferences. One question that I was constantly asked was "what is it about Steven (and me) that enabled him to cope with being deprived of his liberty for a whole year?" I found myself replying to this question, more and more, by making unformed reference to Steven's love, belief and balls. Those three intrinsic parts of his character served him very well over that year and continue to be the main source of his survival and thriving as an autistic man in a world that can be quite hostile to autistic people. Love, Belief and Balls seemed the obvious title for a blog, especially as the blog was mainly going to be about our experiences in the world of social care.

There have been many times since the original idea of the blog in 2013 that I have questioned where those values come from. They are the values that I have lived my life by, and they are a daily inspiration in living with Steven.

I wanted a better understanding of why they appeal to me so much and where, and how, they were rooted.

Where do the lines that run through these experiences of love, belief and balls originate from?

I started this chapter with a dream, so I'll end with one. This dream was from last night; before I started writing.

I am a contestant on a TV game show. It is a cross between the Anneka Rice vehicle, 'Treasure Hunt', and one of those Bear Grylls survival types of jobbies. The overall mission of the programme is to go on a journey and to collect clues that will lead to a place called 'Future World'. The first programme focuses on assembling the equipment necessary for the journey. I am shocked to discover that my only assistance is to be the box left by Peter Ustinov from the old dream. I am left bemused and unsure where to start with this adventure.

Nicholas Parsons seems a good enough place to start.

2: Nicholas Parsons & Southall

"And now

From Norwich

It's the quiz of the week"

Dee dee dee. Dee dee dee. Dee dee da da da.

Twenty five minutes on from the opening credits, Nicholas Parsons is about to reveal to this week's outstanding winner, the selection of four tempting treats on offer in today's 'Sale Of The Century'. This week's outstanding winner has played a tactical blinder all programme, avoiding the allure of spending some of his hard earned winnings in the five instant sales. This week's outstanding winner has built such an impressive purse that he will be able to afford any of the four goodies that Mr Parsons will shortly unveil.

This week's outstanding winner is my Uncle Bob.

Back in Florence Road, Southall, most of the family has gathered in our house at number 1A and are squatting/crouching/squashing expectantly around our 18 inch Radio Rentals console. The programme was recorded three months ago, so Uncle Bob is one of our group, half in the living room and half preparing to make a quick getaway by the front stairs. The tension isn't eased by our prior knowledge of what Uncle Bob chose as his "life changing prize". I am 13 years old and am feeling grouchy. I've not been home long, having been to Woolworths to purchase the newly released 'Truck on Tyke' by T Rex and, if truth be told, I'd have rather been in my bedroom, practising my Marc Bolan impression in front of the wardrobe mirror. Being a Mark, I feel a natural affinity with Mr Bolan and since 'Telegram Sam'; I've taken to spelling my name 'Marc' on my pencil case and rough book. It hasn't caught on yet. In fact, I was marked down on my history essay for an elementary spelling mistake. All this probably adds to my grouchiness. But it's important to show family solidarity, so my turntable remains sedentary and I sneak a Wagon Wheel from the kitchen and squash up on the sofa next to my Dad. It's a good position from which to watch Auntie Wilky.

Auntie Wilky's natural resting expression tends to be serious. When you get to know her she's actually a good laugh but, catch her unawares and she usually looks serious. If she was in hospital and the doctor said that her condition was serious, you wouldn't be worried because that is her natural state. Since the television recording though, her mood has been different. A Mr Whippy recipe of serious and morose. The mood in our living room, emanating solely from her, is extreme tension.

"Congratulations, Robert. You are this week's outstanding champion. Walk this way, Robert and join me in the Sale Of The Century".

In Florence Road, we are all slightly startled. Uncle Bob isn't Robert. But Nicholas Parsons leans towards the formal. I bet only his closest friends would dare to call him Nick. We pray that Uncle Bob doesn't misread this as a cue for familiarity and respond with "I'm on my way Nick". Due to the nervous atmosphere in the front room, I also don't do my John Inman impression when Nick says "walk this way".

I know that we all want to enjoy this moment. A united pleasure in Uncle Bob's fifteen minutes of fame. But we also have a major mystery to solve, summed up best by my Dad three months ago when Uncle Bob's grand prize was delivered….. "Why the fuck did you choose a….?"

"Our first item today, Robert is a complete new bedroom suite. A sumptuous double bed, roomy wardrobe, spacious chest of drawers, feminine dressing table and the all - important ottoman. All in a matching shade of flamingo pink. What would your wife say to this, Robert?"

Instinctively we all turn to look at Auntie Wilky, but we all know exactly what she would say. Auntie Wilky isn't flamingo pink. Her coats are religiously fawn and her pinafore dresses are either grey or navy blue. It may be exaggerating but I assume that all hell would have to freeze over first before Auntie Wilky would give house room to a flamingo pink bedroom combination.

Nick picks up the vibe from a few hundred miles away.

"I can see you're having doubts, Robert. Never mind. We still have three other goodies to tempt you with. Let's move on to our second item in this week's Sale of the Century. Robert, how about six nights for two people in an idyllic country cottage in Split, the capital of Yugoslavia? A second honeymoon perhaps, Robert?"

We laugh nervously at Nicholas's slightly saucy joke but we know deep down that it's another non-starter. For the last fifteen years, Auntie Wilky and Uncle Bob have had two holidays a year. The first week in May and the last week in September. Carefully planned to avoid potential school holidays and hordes of schoolkids. And their venue was the same every year: at Jess and Cyril's bed and breakfast in West Wittering. The best and only condition that Auntie Wilky would put on a holiday venue is that "it's like a home from home" and nobody would ever be able to convince her that Split could be as homely as Southall. Or West Wittering.

"Not impressed, Robert? Let's move on...."

Is Nicholas getting a little irritated? Has an edge crept in to his customary charm?

The first chorus of Please Release Me comes over the airwaves.

"Our third item, Robert is tickets for the entire family to attend a live performance by Mr Englebert Humperdink at the world famous, Talk Of The Town".

The middle aged ladies in the studio audience are in danger of losing their shit.

"This superb prize includes dinner at a top London restaurant, hosted by one of Britain's greatest singers and light entertainers, the great man himself….."

Do other people in the family know about Auntie Wilky's secret? A few years earlier we were going shopping and Auntie Wilky asked me to fetch her handbag from her bedroom (grey, with a navy blue trim on the pillowcases). I searched high and low and finally opened her wardrobe door, which revealed a large poster of Englebert sellotaped on the inside. His orange shirt was unbuttoned pretty much to the waist and there was a serious amount of chest hair on show. Serious, sensible Auntie Wilky was a fangirl. I'd never seen her in that light before and it shook me to my core. An eight year old's lesson that people aren't always who you expect them to be. It raised the dilemma of whether I should let on, but I hadn't the first clue how to, so I kept it to myself for the time being. Well, until this chapter actually.

Did Nicholas know that he was offering Robert's wife a ticket to heaven? Did Robert realise what was being handed to him on a plate? Did he not clock how many years and years' worth of marital brownie points were in the bag? Did every one of us in Florence Road avoid Auntie Wilky's eye as Please Release Me faded out during the bridge? I think we were afraid to see that she might be crying.

"It's a wonderful prize Nicholas, but would you mind if we pressed on please?"

"Okay Robert. You've rejected the gorgeous bedroom collection. You've turned your back on a romantic getaway to Yugoslavia. You've said no to a once in a lifetime experience and put Englebert Humperdink back in his record sleeve. That means, Robert, you will be taking home tonight…."
The TV switched off. A power cut. The 1973 three day week refused to extend itself. Dad thumped the top of the television and Auntie Rose bumped into the hostess trolley in the dark.

A few weeks before transmission, I found myself sitting with my Mum and Uncle Bob in a turquoise blue VW camper van that was parked outside our house. Mum was being encouraging and making Uncle Bob a cup of tea and a cheese sandwich and telling him that every cloud had a silver lining and he wouldn't have been able to make himself a cuppa and a cheese sandwich at the Talk of the Town.

I tried to join in with this blatant "always look on the bright side of life" Neary routine and was lying down on the put-you-up. It's nice, but nobody in their right mind could ever describe the camper van as a home from home. Auntie Wilky had never had to collapse her dining room table to turn it into a bed.

I broke the silence:

"But you can't drive, Uncle Bob".

"I know, Marky".

Mum scolded me:

"Mark. It'll be alright when the dust settles".

I persevered:

"Why did you choose the camper van, Uncle Bob?"
"I don't know, Marky".

Mum brought this enquiry to a close:

"Eat your sandwich, Bob. I know my sister and this will all blow over soon".

Uncle Bob and I exchanged a look that said, "She's doing her best, but she's lying".

Uncle Bob decided to go into full confession mode:

"I froze. I'd concentrated so hard on the questions: I was like a wet rag. I hadn't even thought that I might win and get to the Sale of the Century round".

I believed him. I spent hours with Uncle Bob before the recording, helping him prepare for his big night. Capital cities in Africa. FA Cup winning goal scorers from the 1950s and 1960s. The hits of T Rex. We covered all bases. Except what he would do if he got to the final round of 'Sale of the Century'. Perhaps it was his modesty that everyone liked about him: he didn't expect to win. We all tried to take our share of the responsibility. I had failed as his coach. If I had remembered my secret about the wardrobe door, I could have communicated that to him in some way. Mum blamed herself. She had encouraged him to go on the show. She knew that Uncle Bob was a huge fan of the show and of Nicholas Parsons more generally. She chastised herself and said that she should have got him tickets to be in the studio audience for 'Just a Minute' for his birthday instead. We tried to atone for ourselves but it didn't cut much ice when, every time we looked out of the window or left the house, we had to navigate the camper van parked randomly in our front garden.

Uncle Bob died in 1984, eleven years later. My Mum was right. Things did blow over. The camper van remained parked in the front garden for eleven years. It became a useful addition to put up unexpected guests in. It acted as a spill over room at family parties. I used it as a quiet space when I was studying for my O Levels. Family members who could drive would frequently pop over and take Auntie Wilky and Uncle Bob on a little run out to Windsor. In the summer we would sit there and listen to Nicholas Parsons on the wireless. For durability and flexibility of use, it beat a flamingo pink dressing table.

It's 2019. All the people who had crammed into our living room that day in 1973 to share Uncle Bob's triumph, except my sister and me, have died. Nicholas Parsons is still going though, but he's probably forgotten the part he played in the Neary/Worley family history. It's been 46 years, after all.

My trip down memory lane is cut short by Steven. Steven is my 29 year old son. He is autistic and has learning disabilities. Each day, he likes to take a photograph out of one of the albums and throws himself into an incredibly detailed commentary of the said picture. One photo can take up to an hour. Who is in the photo? What is everyone wearing? What are the titles of all the books and the videos on the shelves? What music were we listening to in the photo? What had we eaten for lunch that day? Where are the people who were missing from the snap? Steven anchors the date of the photo in three ways: whose class was he in at school, where did we go that year for holiday, and who was on that year's Christmas Top of the Pops? In his chronology, 1998 isn't 1998.

It's Gilbert Best's class, a chalet in Devon and the year of Cher, Fat Les and The Tamperer.

Today, he's extracted a photo from 1995. We both remember the day well. To him it's: Maggie's class, a caravan in Burnham and Take That and The Outhere Brothers. To me, it's the day that I smelled the ghost of my Dad. In the picture, Steven and I are having a lark in the Uxbridge open air pool. It is mid-summer but we are the only two people in the water. The grey clouds give the game away, as does the man wearing a mac in the background. Nobody in their right mind would brave an unheated pool on a day like today. Even the ticket attendant checked with me three times that we actually wanted to swim and not just go on the bouncy castle. Cut from stout cloth, my son and I take the plunge. No sitting by the side, dangling our feet in the water for 20 minutes. A running jump. With a heroic yawp whilst we were in mid-air. And then stunned silence for the next five minutes whilst we acclimatise. Steven likes to sing medleys in swimming pools, but it's a good 10 minutes before we can find the breath to give Uxbridge (or just the chap in the mac) our Adam & The Ants mash up.

After half an hour we've had enough. When you've turned a bluey mauve, only a mug of Bovril and a hot dog can bring you back from your hallucinogenic trip. And then it happened. As I was climbing the steps out of the pool, the smell smacked me around the face. The smell of my Dad in his charcoal Speedos in Southall open air pool circa 1966. This time the smell was coming from me. An odd but loaded smell. Was it a generic smell of middle aged men emerging from outside pools? Unfortunately, being the sole swimmers that morning, there were no other middle aged men around to test my theory out on. No 40-year-old just about to somersault from the high diving board whom I could ask politely, "Excuse me Sir. Do you mind if I just sniff your trunks before your forward dive with pike?"

I became slightly obsessed with this smell. In fact, it opened a door to a whole collection of aged smells. Some long forgotten. Most of them very much of their time. Nice smells and putrid smells collide in the power of their resonance. Weirdly, for someone who embraces all shades of melancholia, this doesn't feel like a nostalgic thing. Some of the smells may be attached to things that have been lost but this doesn't feel about loss. It's as present tense as it is past.

Camper vans?

Don't worry. I'm getting there.

Have you ever had that sensation when you wake up one morning, bolt upright, with an idea that is so clear that you can touch it? Smell it even. Well, it was like that this morning. I woke up knowing that I had to retrace my steps to the 1998 Devon holiday and immerse myself into the icy saltwater filled tank that is Shoalstone open air pool. And to take

Steven, and although he's not 30 until next year, to see if he now has the same smell as generations of Neary men.

One thing that I know with absolute clarity is that something would be waiting for us at Shoalstone Lido. I've no idea what, but something is there that I need to see and hear and touch and smell. Something for the past, the present and the future.

And the only other thing I know with total certainty is that the only way I'm going to travel to Devon is in a camper van.

The fact that I can't drive is a minor inconvenience.

3. Books

August 1967. The Summer of Love. I am eight.

I am feeling a little lonely.

I have quite a few friends at school and I have one friend that I would call my best friend – Trevor Callier. We are suitably matched. We can do the same things that our other friends do (Tag, What's The Time Mister Wolf) but we are considered weirdos because we do other stuff too. I have my collection of "It books" that my head is regularly buried in. And Trevor has a pet unicorn. Nobody has ever seen the unicorn, but nobody questions its existence either. It's taken as a given in Trevor's life, as much as his signed photograph of Jimmy Greaves. Trevor was unfortunately unable to attend my eighth birthday party a few months earlier, because he had to take the unicorn grazing on Norwood Green. It was a big blow, but entirely reasonable in my eyes. And on the last day of school a week ago, Trevor announced that he would be unavailable for the entire six-week holiday due to the fact that both his parents had full-time jobs so his duty for the long vacation was to house sit the unicorn.

I've always been comfortable with my own company. After all, I had my It books for companionship. Woolworths sold a pack of four rough books in four different colours for sixpence. I used the red one to write down the Radio

Luxembourg Top 30 every Tuesday night. The blue one was used for my record of each game of Southall Football club and the endless statistics I used to compile (How many players wore the number seven shirt that season). In the yellow book, I used to develop my own television schedules. It was daily from 4pm to 10pm but was always a bit top-heavy with extra episodes of 'Crossroads' and 'Adam Adamant'. I had never found a consistent theme for the green books. I toyed with poetry and even had a few weeks designing new crisp packets, but nothing really took off. Not until the summer of 1967.

Without Trevor around, the school holiday started to drag. I invented a game called "Balls". I had a collection of about twenty balls of varying sizes. I would load them into my Mum's washing basket, sit at the top of our back stairs with the back door open and then turn the basket upside down so that the balls rolled down the stairs and across the garden lawn. In my spare, green It book, I would then compile in-depth league tables tracking the success and failure of each ball. Promotion and relegation issues rested on fundamentals like speed, trajectory and whether Uncle Bob had left the lawnmower out of the shed. My favourite ball was a medium sized green and blue striped ball and I had no qualms about rigging the results so that it invariably came out as top of the league. It was an interesting diversion, but lacking in long-term life fulfilment. I needed to get out more.

In 1967, my Auntie Rose had a cleaning job for our local GP, Doctor Pragnell. He also had a private practice which he ran from his imposing home in Osterley Park Road, just opposite the library. The family epitomised, to eight year old me, unheard-of wealth; for three weeks every August they decamped to their holiday home on the Isle of Wight and took part in Cowes Week Regatta. The appendicitis rate in Southall was high enough to afford them a yacht and the stories went that Mrs. Pragnell entertained everyone from Princess Margaret to Mike and Bernie Winters for sumptuous summer teas. Auntie Rose was retained during their break to go in each Monday and Thursday to keep the house all ship shape and Bristol fashion. One Monday morning she asked if I would like to go with her. A common expression amongst my family if ever they ventured beyond their normal anchors was, "Oooh. It's like another world". That first day at Doctor Pragnell's, with each of his 18 rooms (18 rooms!) wasn't just another world. It was another galaxy. The huge kitchen had four Welsh dressers, resplendent with every piece of crockery imaginable and some whose purpose I couldn't imagine at all. Twice a week, Auntie Rose would dutifully take down each piece and dust every last saucer. Then there was the imposing lounge with three extra-long Chesterfields. They were the same colour as my dad's Doctor Marten boots, only more expertly polished. A room I tried to avoid was the scary consulting room, with the antique oversized desk; the bare examination bed and a solitary skeleton, terrifyingly intimidating and standing to attention by the bay window. It took until the last week of the holiday for me to summon up the courage and to shake hands with the skeleton.

But it was upstairs that the house really came into its own. On that first day, I opened one door and it revealed a children's play room, the same size as our entire flat. I cried. I think it was my first experience of being overwhelmed by something so incomparable to my regular experience. Doctor Pragnell had two daughters and a very 1960s attitude to gender appropriate playthings, so it was very girly, but that didn't seem to matter to me. There was a dolls' house, about half the size of one of the Welsh dressers and it had a swimming pool in the roof garden. Gallingly, considering my daily practice of trying to accustom myself to the icy waters of Southall open-air pool, this swimming pool was heated. The doll's house had servants' quarters. And real electricity. If the doll's house was the centrepiece of this magical kingdom, there were many other delights. The full size rocking horse that I wasn't tall enough to mount on my own. The wigwam. The activity table with more colours of plasticine I'd ever imagined before or since. Auntie Rose came into the room behind me as I stood frozen to the spot, eyes agog and mouth agape, and told me that I could play with anything that was unlikely to break, and I had to swear that I would put everything back exactly as I had found it. I thought that I had stumbled into an episode of 'The Flowerpot Men' and the secret adventures that Bill and Ben got up to whenever the gardener went for his lunch.

I missed it the first day that I was there, but when I went back on the Thursday, I noticed a small child-sized door at the back of the playroom. I thought that it was a cupboard initially, but upon opening it I realised that you had to crawl through it and it led to another room. It led to a library. With hundreds of children's books. I had found a spiritual home.

I was so immersed in my discovery that I hadn't heard Auntie Rose calling out for me and I was catapulted from my wonderment when her head appeared through the little door. She wasn't overweight by any stretch of the imagination, but she struggled to squeeze through the miniature opening. I loved that. What kind of genius would build a room that was only accessible to little people? It did bother me thinking about how they had managed to build all those splendid bookcases. Did they build them outside of the room and force them through, or (and this was pre Ikea or MFI days) did they employ a team of dwarves and assemble them in the room itself? I wouldn't have had a clue where to start with such engineering conundrums. I spent an hour just taking books off the shelves, smelling them, stroking their spines and making a mental list of which ones I would read first. I asked Auntie Rose if I could take one home with me. She wasn't sure and gave me a whole list of dos and don'ts. This seemed perfectly reasonable to me, as I knew that whenever my Dad wanted to rest down his cup of tea, it would be any coaster in a storm. I think she was pushing it a bit with her last two demands though: Don't have a book out whilst I'm eating custard; and if the house burns down, make sure that I rescue the book before I rescue my sister. The sense of responsibility felt so daunting that I almost left the books where they were. If I had, I probably wouldn't be writing this book.

The first book I chose was 'David Copperfield'. I'm not sure why. It wasn't an informed decision. I wasn't familiar with the works of Dickens. I didn't associate our rendition of Food Glorious Food at harvest assembly with the author of the book I was holding. Auntie Rose had shouted out to tell me that my haslet sandwich was ready for lunch, so I'm sure I just grabbed the first book that came to hand. I read it solidly over the next few days. I didn't see daylight. If Trevor Callier had turned up and asked me to go for a walk with his unicorn, I would probably have declined. I was frightened by Uriah Heep; amused by Mr Micawber; enchanted by Dora. I cried when Steerforth drowned in Yarmouth and vowed to cross Yarmouth off our list of potential holiday destinations. I encountered people like Peggotty, whom I already knew well. She was like a lot of my neighbours from Florence Road, all rolled into one. But characters like Betsy Trotwood were a completely delightful mystery. The story began to impact on my real life and I started to fret about scenarios that I had never given a moment's thought to before. How would I manage if my Dad died and my Mum remarried a total bounder? These sorts of questions had never arisen during my repeated viewings of 'Camberwick Green'.

The biggest opening that David Copperfield afforded me was to teach me that life existed in a previous century. The 1800s. I am sure that up until that point, I had assumed that the small Southall world that I knew had started sometime around 1920. I had vaguely heard of Darwin, but my timeline had been sketchy. He could have been talking about the roaring twenties. I had been vaguely interested whenever my uncles compared their wartime experiences, but I don't think I had slotted these stories into any specific period of time. It was around chapter ten that I said to my Mum,

"Mum, do we know anyone who was around at the same time as David Copperfield?"

She immediately mentioned my Nan (her mother), but as she had died when I was two, she wasn't a very firm, fleshed-out figure in my mind. Then she brought up our next door neighbour, Mrs Eden, who in 1967 was probably in her late seventies. I did a quick calculation and worked out that if Dora Copperfield had lived, she would possibly be the same age as Mrs Eden was now. That rough piece of arithmetic certainly firmed out a timeline in my head. I was brand new to paying attention to this sort of historical chronology and linking our elderly neighbour to my new-found fictional heroine seemed incredible to me. I wanted to go at once and interview Mrs Eden about the diseases of her early life, but Mum warned against this. There was a suggestion of youthful tragedy in Mum's warning, so I didn't pursue my research. If Mrs Eden's twin brother had died an early death from rickets, I was never to find out. But from that day on, I held Mrs Eden in a new, higher esteem, purely on account of her living a life that had straddled two centuries.

One other thing happened that summer that, looking back, changed my view of the world. It must have been a week or so after my discovery of the library at Doctor Pragnell's. I had finished David Copperfield and moved on to my first taste of Will Scott's excellent series of books with 'The Cherrys of River House'. They were similar in format to the Famous Five and the Secret Seven, except that the adult Cherrys were also involved in the solving of the mysteries. The children were "the littles" and the adults were "the bigs". Inspired by these tales of multi-generational derring-do, I suggested to my Mum that we set out on an adventure one afternoon. I wanted a Cook's tour of Southall whilst being told stories from my family's and my town's past. My Mum was game and brought Auntie Rose along for the ride and to push my sister, now eighteen months old, in her pushchair.

We spent a lot of time by the gasworks. Both of the women had stories about Spencer Street, which ironically was the road where Trevor Callier lived. I was shown the house that was used for the filming of a Diana Dors' movie and told how, from that fifteen minutes of fame, the family who owned the house had developed ideas above their station. Blinds instead of curtains. The audacity of it! Mum reminded me that my Dad worked for a painter and decorator when he was in his early teens. She pointed out a house and told me that back in 1941, my Dad had been up a ladder clearing out the guttering and when he returned a day later to finish the job, the house had been bombed and had been turned into a pile of rubble. I was shown the house that Cleo Laine had grown up in. We passed Mr Huggins' greengrocers' shop that, during the war had done a roaring trade in black market bananas. All these stories brought about an even bigger revelation than the fact that there had been a century before the current one, populated by people that I had a connection with. It was that all the people in my life had lived a life before I came along. My Mum had been a Beryl. Auntie Rose had been a plain Rose Worley without any title. I hope that's not as egotistical as it sounds. I was only eight at the time. At that age, you only see people in relation to you; the fact that they'd had experiences outside of me was a game changer. The story of Dad's brush with death (admittedly remote) blew my mind.

We ended our afternoon magical mystery tour with a trip to the café in Western Road. It was probably to change Jayne's nappy, but the cherry cola and the toasted teacake were very welcome. I was away with the fairies, and trying to process all the history that I had learned in the last three hours. Scott McKenzie was on the jukebox singing his number one hit, 'San Francisco'. The bigs were discussing flower power. Auntie Rose was doubtful. People with bells around their necks and flowers in their hair were crossing a red line of decency, in her opinion. My Mum, twelve years younger than her sister, found the hippy movement quite exciting and had already treated herself to a cheesecloth blouse from Taplins.

Life moves on. Roughly one hundred years separated David Copperfield and Scott McKenzie and those two worlds wouldn't recognise each other physically. However, if I tried hard enough, I might be able to imagine Betsy Trotwood pitching up at Woodstock. After all, as my Mum had said about the hoity-toity family in Spencer Street: "People are just people, Rose, at the end of the day".

I changed that summer. I discovered the realness of books and the present tense of history.

And to think, if Trevor Callier never had a unicorn, none of that would have happened.

4: Amersham Workhouse

1873

"Ah, Doctor. Have you seen the pauper in bed 174?"

"Yes. Worley. The end will come soon. The man has fallen into a state of hallucination and incoherent rambling."

"The man has been rambling for the past ten years. Tell me something new. I shall begin preparations for his final passing."

"Give him no time Matron. All sense has deserted him. All I could understand from his babble is that he wishes to go to Seer Green. He was most insistent. Poor man. The delusions from pain."

"The man is a fool, Doctor. I will forewarn two of the pauper women to remain alert to the necessity of laying him out."

"It will not be long. I will take my leave now Matron."

It was the mention of Seer Green that pricked her attention. But she knew not better to draw attention to herself. Having been brought up in Chalfont St Giles, Sarah was all too aware of the stories about the neighbouring village. She had occasion to visit there twice before on errands for her mother and the fear of God had been planted in her before her excursion. The men were all wild like pack dogs, all illiterate inbreeds; and the women were an indelible stain on their homes and families. Do not speak to them. Do not look them in the eye. Deliver your lace to the schoolrooms and return home immediately.

But Sarah found her fancy tickled.

On that first visit to Seer Green, Sarah was shocked to find herself move from a terror that had kept her awake for two consecutive nights, to a startling joy, very quickly. The fear of God was a brief visitor and Sarah wondered afterwards, how her mother could have reached such illogical conclusions. It must have been that her mother's recollections of Seer Green had come from a time many years previous, when the village had been irreligious. Her mother had shown an understandable maternal instinct towards her daughter and wanted nothing more than her safety.

The first building that Sarah noticed was the Baptist Church in Potkiln Lane. It was not a Sunday, but the building offered a Christian sense of welcome. Two young boys were tending to the church grounds. They sang as they toiled. They were unkempt, but that was surely the results of such hard labour for some so young. Turning the corner at Potkiln Lane, Sarah, saw for the first time, the cherry orchard. She held her stomach, as that first sighting took her breath away. She had never seen anything so huge and so beautiful in all of her twelve years. The colours hurt her eyes, with such glorious colours with which to fashion a duchess's frock. The smell of the fruit made her giddy with its richness. Sarah thought of the grocer bringing her mother's weekly grocery delivery every Thursday and there was nothing to match the array of colours and aromas that enveloped her. Men, women and children struggled to carry the large tin tubs full to the brim with the pickings from the Orchard. Sarah contemplated a life where every day brought her into contact with a bountiful harvest of wares. For a few moments, Sarah thought that she might faint, overcome by the waves of the glorious bouquets.

Sarah sat down on the grass and helped herself to some water from the one hundred and forty foot public well, known to the villagers as the Wide Place. On the edge of the Green was a grand but small building and she noticed that several of the men were carrying their buckets to this establishment. Despite her mother's stern warnings of not speaking to a single soul, Sarah enquired of a young girl as to what the men were doing. She was informed that the men were transporting their day's harvest to Mr Lofty, the baker from Orchard Road. The majority of the fruit would be loaded on to carts and driven by the men to Covent Garden Market in London but the wares of Mr Lofty were famous all over Buckinghamshire and Seer Green had been afforded the affectionate name of Cherry Pie Village. Sarah didn't think she had ever witnessed a more soul-lifting scene.

After delivering her lace to the schoolhouse, Sarah decided to take a different route home and here she encountered her first scene of that day that gave substance to her mother's words. She passed the Jolly Cricketers public house and was chilled by the sight of the toothless, loud men sat outside on old wooden crates. She did not recognise any of these faces and realised that they were not the men she had seen earlier, labouring away in the orchard. Next to the public house were the brickfields and the landscape was taken over by similar-looking men, many of them in a shocking state of undress. There were a few women too, but acting in a manner with the male drinkers that was unbecoming. And some children, presumably the offspring of the imbibers, played marbles with an aggression that filled the beery air and compelled Sarah to run the rest of her journey home.

It was 1873 again and Sarah knew that it wasn't her place to attend to the ailing inmates of the workhouse, but the mention of Seer Green had rekindled those memories of ten years earlier and the starkly contrasting pictures she had stored during that walk to the schoolhouse. She was also taken with the thought, the tease, of discovering whether Mr Worley had been one of the men gaily working in the cherry orchard, or one of the debauched revellers drinking themselves to hell. Keenly aware of her own pride and her struggles with the shame of becoming an inmate herself, Sarah was blind to the possibility that the circumstances pertaining to William Worley's admission might not be too dissimilar to her own. Besides, in her mind, she was a woman of twenty two who had temporarily fallen on hard times; William Worley was facing imminent death at seventy two having been an inmate of the workhouse for the past fourteen years. With the same pluck that she had displayed as a twelve-year-old girl, Sarah determined to seek out Mr Worley; and if that provoked the displeasure of the Master or the Matron, then so be it.

Sarah had never seen a man who was in such colour before. William Worley lay on a sack-covered bed, wearing a threadbare vest and gruesome knee-length breeches. He was, on the whole, black. His ablutions had not been attended to, so much of that black was dirt. But it did not take long for Sarah to realise that beneath the black of dirt, there was the black of rot. William Worley's limbs had decayed to the point where his extremities looked like charred sticks. And amidst the black hue, there were blazing patches of red sores, angry and oozing. Sarah covered her mouth. She wanted to retch at the smell. She doubted whether she had the bravery to kneel by his bedside. Astonishingly, despite the horror of pain that Sarah couldn't even begin to imagine, William Worley seemed to be sleeping. There didn't appear to be any orderlies about, so Sarah cautiously sat down on the floor beside Mr Worley's bed. Partly to avoid looking at the dying wretch, Sarah started to take in her surroundings. Those first few minutes must have been muted in her head, because Sarah suddenly became aware of the sounds. An imbecile in the next bed, possibly the same age as herself, was repeatedly striking his head against the metal bed frame. He uttered no words as he beat out his rhythmic torture. An elderly man in the bed opposite was biting into a piece of old rope. As black as William Worley was, this man was yellow. His still concentration on his biting was occasionally broken by a spasm and a cry that Sarah thought could have come from meeting the Devil himself. The final inmate in the room was sitting up. Compared to the others he seemed almost well. Then Sarah noticed the blood stained blanket half covering him and saw that he was chiselling into an undressed wound with his long, ragged finger nails. He never winced. He was beyond pain.

Sarah trembled and doubted she had the courage to stay a moment longer.

"I want to go to Seer Green. One last time."

William Worley had woken and abruptly seized Sarah's wrist. She had never felt more afraid. She wasn't sitting with a man. He was a diseased animal. He saw her fear.

"Just one more time. My kiddies."

Sarah collected her senses. The fear evaporated for a brief moment.

"I went to Seer Green once. Ten years ago. It was heavenly. Will you tell me all about it?"

William Worley let go of Sarah's arm. He held his own instead. He was struggling for breath. Sarah noticed a single tear.

"I'll go and get you something to give you a wash. Then you can tell me about your life in Seer Green. I'd like that."

Sarah knew that she had to have her wits about her. Although she had been an inmate for four days only, she knew that there were rules. And very clear positions of power; and jobs to be carried out. It would not be seen as productive use of her time to be spent sitting with a dying man, indulging his final moments in sentimental whimsy. But she also felt that, although she found it unpleasant to look at him, she was interested in him and she suspected that it had been many years since anyone had been interested in the life of William Worley. Could she provide companionship and solace, whilst avoiding the wrath of the Master.

As luck would have it, the senior officials at the workhouse had very little time or enthusiasm for this dark, remote part of the institution in the infirmary. The doctor was not expected to attend for another three days and it was doubtful whether Mr Worley would survive that long. The Master was fully occupied with supervising the work of the able inmates and dealing with the intrusions of the Board of Guardians. Matron liked her drink and on most days was ensconced in her quarters from late afternoon. As normal day to day life in the workhouse continued, Sarah found that she had some measure of freedom; certainly she could spend about three hours each day with William Worley. If asked, she could say that she was collecting the gruel bowls to return to the kitchen. Although it was never mentioned that she and William didn't have many days left for their final visit to Seer Green together, they silently acknowledged that the visit would take place from a decrepit, infection-ravaged bed.

Extracts from a notebook found after the death, in March 1881 of Sarah Foresley, aged twenty-nine in Amersham Workhouse:

"William Worley senior was born in Seer Green, Buckinghamshire, in 1801. He was incredibly proud of his family's connection to the village, which dated back to the mid-1600s. He remembers as a boy, his father relating the family history and instilling in him the pride the family could take, in having built this small village into the reasonably prosperous place it is today.

William Worley talked about early ambitions, although he didn't see his hopes and plans for the future as ambitions. As a woman from a very different background from Mr Worley's, I was intrigued by what many may see as humble ambition. I've never met anyone with such a strong sense of place before, and a duty, and commitment towards that place. I can see that it was partly about honouring the family history, but he also seemed to embody a patriotism, in a much smaller way, about a village rather than a whole country. I was brought up in a neighbouring village, but had never felt the same connection with place. This was probably because my family never had the length of connection that the Worleys had. For William Worley, his overriding motivation was to continue that connection, whilst building something of his own in the process.

The day that I visited Seer Green, when I was twelve, I wouldn't have seen William Worley in either the cherry orchard or the pub. From the time that he was twelve, Mr Worley worked in the village sawpit, labouring for long hours in the timber yards, sawing up the logs in readiness for the Seer Green chair factory in Pondstiles.

In 1824, when he was twenty-three years old, William Worley married Rachel Darvill, a local lacemaking girl who was one year his senior. Over the course of the next fifteen years, they produced eight children and quite remarkably, only one of them died in infancy.

Sadly, whilst in labour with their eighth child in 1839, Rachel died. The baby survived and was named Rachel in her mother's memory. William Worley was left with seven children to bring up, and it is here that the community spirit of Seer Green really came into its own. Some of the children went to live with other villagers. In fact, two of the middle children were taken in by Mr Lofty the baker whom I had seen that day many years earlier. William Worley kept the youngest children in his care and by 1851, Ephrahim who was then fifteen and Rachel junior who was then twelve were living with him at Fly Farm in the village where William Worley was working as an agricultural labourer.

In the year after Rachel's death, William Worley had his first encounter with the law and he received a six-month prison sentence for larceny. It may have been this event that accelerated the initial break-up of the family, although most of the children returned to live with Mr Worley upon his release. However, in 1851, William Worley broke the law again and possibly because it was his second burglary offence, this time he received a sentence of ten years. In our conversations we talked about this time and Mr Worley had very little to say about what drove him to crime.

"You keep on, keeping on", was all he could say.

It was not for me to pass judgment as I have not been in the position of having to bring up seven children by myself, but to lose your family for the act of stealing some potatoes seems very harsh to me.

The ten year gaol sentence was the final nail in the coffin for the family staying together. It was difficult for William Worley to talk about the consequences of his time in prison, but I got the impression that he had very little contact with his seven children after his final release. I do know that he never returned to Seer Green after jail and he lived on his own in lodgings in Stanwell. It was there that times became very hard and he was admitted to Amersham Workhouse in the autumn of 1861. I write this journal in 1873 and he has been here to this day.

I last saw William Worley on 22nd November 1873. We had kept each other company for four days. The next morning I was helping some of the pauper women prepare breakfast and my work was interrupted by the sight through the window, of two men carrying a covered body to the mortuary. Nothing was said. No names were mentioned, but I knew in my heart that it was William Worley. Later that week, I took myself to the church for some silent contemplation. Until that day, I had never had cause to visit a pauper's grave. The graves were unmarked and it pained me greatly that I couldn't find Mr Worley's exact resting place. I sat down by what looked like the rawest mound of earth and recited a short prayer.

Some days later I was tasked with a chore that led me to walk down by the river. I remember how William Worley had told me about taking his son William paddling in the pond at Seer Green. I cannot say that he smiled as he recounted this moment, but I did, for the only time in those four days, get a touch of the man's contentment.

At the river, I made a small boat out of some leaves and wrote a brief message that I placed in the boat before pushing it off.

I wanted to bestow, in my humblest way, one last honour on William Worley.

My note read:

"Mr. William Worley. Husband and Father. You kept on, keeping on."

5. Shoalstone Pool

2019

"Echo Beach, far away in time.

Echo Beach, far away in time".

Oh Martha and the Muffins. Thank you. You have been a staple of our holiday compilation cassette tapes since our first family holiday with Steven in 1997. Compilation cassette tapes may seem a bit passé in these days of streaming and Spotify, but Steven being Steven, if we do something once that floats his boat, he has an expectation that we do exactly the same thing forever more. Twenty-two years on from Burnham on Sea and it's bloody difficult to find a hire vehicle that has a built-in cassette player; but to get around that modern extinction we have one of the support workers allocated to nurse a ghetto blaster on his lap for the entire journey. We have some Boney M, some Bay City Rollers and some Lyte Funky Ones, but Martha, your anthem is the one sure-fire hit record to get a camper van full of Cowley men singing at the tops of their voices.

Only today, we are not going on holiday. Three years ago, Steven announced that he didn't want to go on holidays anymore. His reasoning – "Holidays get a bit busy." I'm dead proud of him for spotting that and being able to verbalise it.

I'm sad, of course, because it has meant the end of an annual family holiday, but am chuffed at the same time that he has worked out a way to articulate something that he has found problematic. As a little kid, he always enjoyed a caravan holiday in a Haven/Hoseseasons/Pontins type of site. But the very nature of a holiday park meant that the risk of sensory overload followed by an overwhelming meltdown was always present. It took twenty-six years but Steven eventually worked out an explanation for his distress whilst on holidays and I like how 'a bit busy' sums it up quite succinctly.

So, it is not a full-on, seven days' holiday. Instead, we are having an overnight stay in Paignton and tomorrow morning we will take the camper van on a little run out to Shoalstone open air pool. To sniff trunks. This will be our third visit to the glorious old pool that is cut into the sea at Brixham. The first time was in 1998 and contained a physical shock that I had long forgotten, that happens when your body reacts in bewilderment to being plunged into freezing cold water. Steven and I had held hands and jumped in. It had been several minutes before we had found the breath to speak.

We tried to recapture the experience in 2015 when we hired a cottage in Torquay, but Steven was much wiser this time and his wincing descent into the water took forever. Our team of Nigerian support workers had never known such cold before, but manfully waded out to neck height in an attempt to be encouraging. It did prompt a mini meltdown though:

"Dad. My willy's gone. Steven Neary's willy hasn't gone forever and ever?"

Steven always talks about himself in the third person, but in this instance he could have been expressing the fear of the whole group. Half an hour later, after getting changed, we were still having to reassure Steven Neary, in a packed ice cream parlour, that his willy hasn't gone forever and ever. Our platitudes were not really working, because Steven Neary's willy, like everyone else's willies, still hadn't come back yet.

As Martha and the Muffins fade out and Katrina and the Waves kick in, I realise that we have all slipped into silence. Steven has polished off a packet of salt and vinegar Chipsticks. The guys have stopped arguing about the political situation back in Nigeria. I have stopped worrying about the possibility of the hotel breakfast not serving fried bread. And nobody is fretting about their willies disappearing. We have nothing to say. It is heaven. Steven breaks the quiet:

"Hello man. What's your name, man? You're a man called?"

He mutters something to himself that sounds like "willing", and grinning broadly, returns his attention to accompanying Katrina on the vocals:

"I'm walking on sunshine and don't it feel good. Hey."

We all turn around.

"Who was he talking to?"

"Must have been another driver, passing us."

"I feel alive. I feel the love. I feel alive. That's really rich,"

We have arrived. Paignton. Steven Neary announces that he is very happy. Sybil Fawlty used to pop over to Paignton for a round of golf with the girls. Steven likes the affirmation of knowing that other people have done things that he does.

Shit. No fried bread. Bloody hash browns.

"We can do you extra mushrooms."

"No thanks. But you could stick a slice of bread in the frying pan? I'll pay extra."

"Sorry. It's not on the menu."

This is one of those days when it doesn't feel appropriate to challenge an establishment about their reasonable adjustments policy for disabled customers. Michael swaps Steven's hash brown for a rasher of his own bacon. Teamwork. That's reasonable adjustments.

Shoalstone Pool today feels more like 1998 than 2015. The sun has only just come out for the day. Perhaps we are all in a brave mood. We walk. An army of five soldiers, down the slippery slope into the shallow end. We stop briefly to say goodbye to our willies. We march on, up to our knees. We stop. We look at each other. We are tempting. And goading. Des, who has been holding back slightly, splashes water over our backs. We yelp. We instinctively move backwards until only our ankles are submerged. We stop. Somebody half-heartedly sings Echo Beach. This will not do. How am I going to smell our trunks when we haven't even got them wet yet? I take a run up and throw myself into the water. Michael follows suit. Then the rest of the lemmings hurl themselves to their arctic doom. Even Steven. Once in, you are in and the thought of getting out vanishes. We swim. We jump. We lounge. Steven sings a Steps medley. We have the whole pool to ourselves. We have arrived even before the lifeguards.

After a few minutes we hold a competition – who can swim the furthest underwater? Steven goes first and manages about half a width. We all clap and sing 'We Are The Champions.' Resurfacing, Steven turns to deliver us a thumbs up and says:

"Hello William."

We turn around and notice a strangely-dressed gentleman in his fifties, sitting on the bench behind us. I hadn't spotted him there when we first arrived. He is overdressed for a day on the beach. He's in a suit that has seen better days. He looks as if he got pissed the night before and slept it off at the back of a building site. I want to check if the Paignton Players are putting on 'Oliver', because he would make the perfect Bill Sykes. But he seems affable enough and returns Steven's greeting by name. He lights up an old clay pipe, rebelling against the many no smoking signs that are dotted around the pool perimeter. Thank goodness the lifeguards aren't on duty yet.

After half an hour and with our willies invisible, we decide that we have had enough. I am first out of the changing room and spot the man with the pipe, who is now sitting on the wall outside the cafeteria.

"Good morning", he beckons.

Knowing that Steven will probably want a hot dog and a Bovril, I walk across and sit down next to him on the wall.

"Good morning. You not going for a swim yet?"

"Too cold, Mark. And I wasn't expecting to swim today."

I am not sure how to respond to this. Perhaps he was on his morning constitutional and settled here for the spectator sport of watching six Cowley nincompoops lose their crown jewels. So, I set about squeezing my towel and trunks into my backpack.

"You've got a good lad there."

"I think so."

"He was very amiable to me yesterday."

"Yesterday? Oh, are you staying at the same hotel as us? Did you see him there? Isn't it a bugger about the fried bread?"

"The Hotel? No, it was in your van. He asked me my name."

"The van? Where were you then? On the motorway?"

"Have you lost your marbles? I was in your van. Bloody terrible music."

This feels like an episode of 'Fawlty Towers' with Basil talking completely at cross purposes with one of the guests. I fall into silence again, because frankly, I am not sure whether he is still drunk from the night before. I can't smell drink but you never know.

Steven and the guys emerge from the changing rooms and come and join us. The man with the pipe offers Steven a mint. As is his won't, Steven takes the whole packet.

"Thank you William."

I am struggling to tune in.

"You were in the van with us?"

"I was. Sitting next to that chap with spectacles."

I turn to look at Alan but he isn't paying attention, on account of cleaning the sand off his spectacles.

"And what did you say your name was?"

"William. William Worley."

Chris honks the horn on the camper van and Steven and the support workers get up and amble over. William Worley starts to follow them. I remain rooted to the wall. William Worley notices this and comes back to join me.

"You know who I am?"

"I think so. Yes, I do know who you are. Sorry, it's a bit of a shock."

"Don't see why".

I feel I can start to move my legs again, so we catch up with the rest of the party.

"You wouldn't be going near Seer Green, I suppose? There's a few things, a few people that I would like to see."

"Erm, sure. We can drop you off along the way. If you don't mind, I'll sit in the back with you. There's a lot I'd like to talk to you about."

"Never been much of a talker, me. Rather I'll just come along for the ride."

And we drive off. And we don't say a word to each other during the whole of the four-hour journey. Michael tries to engage him in a conversation about Brexit but he is true to his word and isn't much of a talker. His only response to Michael was:

"You'd better talk to the boy there when you get home" and he gestures towards me.

Chris gets into a bit of a pickle locating Seer Green on the sat nav but eventually we arrive. Steven has been moaning because in the shock of this morning's unusual reunion, we've forgotten to pick up a hot dog from the cafeteria. We pull up in the car park of the Jolly Cricketers, and I get out to let William Worley out by the back door. But when I open the door, he has already left. Without a word.

I have never been to Seer Green before. I had read about it a few years ago when I had been researching my family tree and I guess that in my mind, I had locked the village into the times when the Worley family reigned supreme in the area.

Today, the place looks like any other small, affluent village. A classy cafeteria. A Conservative Club. Four estate agents.

No orchard and no well.

I fancy an early night. I cannot escape the thought that perhaps I had been asleep all day, even though I know that I haven't. It had all happened. As I unpack my bag, my trunks are still wet and Steven is polishing off the last of the mints he had been given by his great-great-great-great-grandfather.

Michael, who was the last man standing to do the night shift has said that he would organise Steven's bath if I wanted to get some shut eye.

"You never said. Who was the man at the pool?"

"The man in the van? Oh, just my great-great-great-grandfather."

"Cool."

I like Michael. He can take throwaway remarks like that completely in his stride.
That was about 9 o'clock. It is 3 o'clock before I start to feel even the remotest bit tired.

My last thought before finally dropping off to sleep is:

"Shit. I forgot to do the smelling of the trunks experiment".

That had been the whole point of the day.

6. Frequencies

I remember just two things from the time spent, studying physics in my first two years at senior school. I am from that generation who, come the third year of their secondary education, dropped several subjects from their curriculum to concentrate on the subjects that we liked, were good at and were going to pursue up to O-level. Physics was the first on my list to receive the heave-ho.

My first memory is of "a force". The physics teacher was a Mr Clark, affectionately known as Nobby Clark, but not to his face. He was a very tall man. And very wide. And very deep, but only in physical stature. One morning he chose six of us from the class and instructed us to form a line at one end of the classroom with arms linked as if we were about to perform a rendition of Auld Lang Syne. Taking off his jacket and rolling up his sleeves, Nobby walked to the other end of the classroom. Positioning himself as if he were in the starting blocks for an Olympic 110 metres hurdles final, Nobby announced:

"I am Newton. You are six atoms. This experiment will show what happens, I say, what happens to atoms, when they come into contact with a force. I am a force."

I forgot to mention that he had the same repetitive speech pattern as Fred Elliott from Coronation Street. With that, he sprang from his blocks and hurtled towards us tiny atoms with his massive belly bouncing like a trampolining Old English Sheepdog. The force got to within two inches of the atoms when we quite reasonably broke our link and scarpered. Nobby careered headlong into the blackboard whilst we atoms shook in a combination of relief, and fear of the retribution heading our way.

Nobby was furious and threatened a week-long detention for any atom that carried on 'behaving like a pathetic weakling.' Back into his starting blocks he went and once again he delivered his script: "I am Newton etc etc…", and once again as he got to within inches of us, instinct took over and for the second time we broke ranks. Crash. The blackboard easel went for a Burton. Nobby was so angry that snot shot from his nostril. Fair play to his creativity, and his determination not to be outdone, Nobby thought of a different way in which to teach us about forces hitting atoms and got us all to bend over. His slipper became the force and our bottoms became the atoms. Thank you, Mr Newton.

My second memory of Mr Clark's physics lessons is even patchier. I do remember that it took several weeks of setting up the experiment and that we were meant to learn something about frequencies. Nearly fifty years later, my knowledge of this vital area of physics is pitiful. I do recall having to construct a Heath Robinson circuit board jobbie. There was a maze of wires that connected a series of knobs that ran around the outside of the board. Once our contraption was complete, our pathway to understanding frequencies should have been clear. We were expected to work out why it was that when you pressed the knob with the sticky label "E" attached, the bulb with the sticky label "H" lit up, whilst the bulbs with the sticky labels "G", "I" and "J" remained dimmed. I didn't know then and I don't know now. Apparently, Nobby reassured us, it was all down to conductors operating on a different frequency. This could have prompted one of the class wags to come out with an Andre Previn joke, but as we had learned from the Newton lesson, Nobby had little capacity for humour when such life-enhancing learning objectives were on the line. One of the girls stuck up her hand and asked why her bulb with the sticky label "C" had lit up and she was sent out to walk around the playground five times. Let's just say, Mr Clark and his young band of atoms were on different frequencies back in 1971 and probably still are in 2019. I know that I am.

Something did register though and I've often found myself pondering questions of frequencies in the years since Featherstone High School. In my professional counselling work, I have seen many people who have been propelled into therapy because they are clearly on a different frequency from the loved one, they have chosen to live their life with. It's what keeps Relate in business. I've encountered many people who glaze over when I press my E knob in an attempt to explain why Sparks were the most underrated band of the Seventies. I have to accept that, not only have I completely missed their H bulb, but every other bulb in their circuit. It's irritating, but I can't really attribute any blame to them. If they don't appreciate the Mael brothers, I know which one of us is losing out. A walk around the playground for you, chum.

My counselling tutor had many mantras. One that has stuck with me is, "There is no place for humour in the counselling room". At the time he said it, I had never been in a counselling room as the therapist, but I was suspicious of his reasoning. Actually, he didn't give any reasoning, which further aroused my suspicions that he was incorrect. Laughter is one circuit board where we quickly learn about each other's frequencies. You either find Billy Connolly funny, or you don't. The bulb lights up, or it stays dark. There is never any midway flickering. In my work, I can turn up the empathy to maximum volume, but if you're on alien frequencies, you ain't going to hear a single word.

It's always been a fascination, but has never been as tested to its limits as it was until after Steven came along. When you find someone whom you love more than your heart can reasonably manage, you expect your frequencies to click like a beginner's jigsaw puzzle. Steven was transparently on a different frequency. Not just from me, but, it seemed at first, from the whole world. It never appeared to bother him, though. Quite the contrary, he was completely at home on his frequency. I learned very early on that there was no point waiting for Steven to join me on my frequency. That wasn't going to happen. I needed to build a whole new circuit board of relating, and then hope, just hope, that I could occasionally light up his bulb.

I don't know how many years I've got left on this mortal frequency, but I'm pretty sure that whenever my final day comes, my greatest source of pride will be the same as it is today. Steven and I have found a frequency that we can connect on; mainly through music, comedy and our shared history. If truth be told, that's how my frequency connects with most people, but with Steven, it's been a magical miracle. And my goodness, am I protective of it. I will fight any person who tries (usually inadvertently) to scramble our frequency.

I wish I were on the same frequency as Steven full-time. I prefer his to mine. It's direct and uncomplicated. It's honest and real. It feels like it comes from a different time, a different age. And it's powerfully intuitive. Mine gets too easily clogged up or diverted off to lesser, insignificant bulbs. It's no coincidence that Steven spotted William Worley before I did. His pathway is unfettered and more open to receiving magic.

In 1879, someone else was struggling with her frequencies. Mary Ann Holloway, for that is what she demanded to be called in those days, had been an in-patient at Hanwell Lunatic Asylum since 1875. In fact the date of admission had been 11th September 1875. The observant doctors had not missed the fact that her arrival at the asylum had been twenty years to the day since she married.

To the doctors and staff, Mary Ann was a source of great puzzlement. What was clearly a case of a mild malaise four years ago had now reached a point where the poor woman was now in the grip of extreme insanity. Brief moments of lucidity had long since passed; the doctors had abandoned any attempt at treatment and were offering nothing more than containment, until her eventual demise. This could not come soon enough, as her increasing acts of violence towards herself and others threatened the efficient running of the hospital. The doctors had discouraged the family from visiting, as a means of alleviating both the patient's and the family's distress; and for everyone's safety Mary Ann was confined to a solitary cell.

Back in 1875, it had all been so different. Mrs Mary Ann Worley, as she was then known and which was her conventional title, had seemed troubled and of a highly nervous state, but she cooperated with the treatment and spoke freely about her life. Slowly, and by careful listening, the ward matron built up an understanding of Mary Ann's malaise, but was perturbed that the telling of her story and the prescribed water treatment only seemed to accelerate her mental decline. That went against all modern thinking and it needed to be considered that perhaps Mary Ann may have been cultivating her nerves. At thirty six years of age, one would have anticipated a full recovery, but Mrs Worley remained a strain on the public purse.

These days, the slightest mention of her home life caused Mary Ann to commit extreme acts of unbecoming aggression. Food was thrown, clothes were torn whenever the family entered the conversation. Mary Ann spent most of her days praying that the good Lord would end her misery as soon as he saw fit.

Mary Ann's life, prior to the asylum, appeared full of contentment. She was married at sixteen to a brick labourer from the neighbouring village. His name was William Worley Junior. Their attraction to each other was simple: Mary Ann adored William's reliability and optimism; William loved Mary Ann's beauty and her commitment to building a loving home. William had big plans, that were slowly forming and of which, he thought it best if he didn't yet speak. He had become tired of working in the brick fields of Seer Green, and wanted to broaden his horizons. He had heard the stories about the new towns, springing up all around London, and he wanted to be part of this excitement. He loved the village that he had grown up in, but if a man is to make his mark on the world, he needs to aim higher than the relative comfort that he already knows. Mary Ann had listened attentively to William's dreams of a better life, but felt torn. She wanted, so much to spend the rest of her days with William; bringing up their children, but why couldn't he be happy with what he had already got? Mary Ann chided herself. They weren't planning on moving to the other side of the world. She would still be able to see her dear mother. If only she could silence these misgivings and share her husband's enthusiasm.

Motherhood proved to be a trying time for Mary Ann. Whilst William pursued his big dreams, Mary Ann struggled to devote herself to her eight children. They were good children, but demanding nonetheless. She lost three other infants and buried her pain with the babies. After her mother passed over, she realised that she had nobody else in the world with whom she could share her sadness. It was during this time of so many losses that Mary Ann began to fully understand what feeling lonely, really meant. As the years passed, Mary Ann lost all interest in herself, her children, her husband, and her home. Her mind became consumed with tormenting thoughts of how she could escape from it all.

There was one day that would be forever locked in Mary Ann's mind, as the day when the world that she knew, ended. And she knew, with bitter irony, that William looked upon the same day, as the day when his new world began. William, full of anticipation, had taken Mary Ann on a short trip where he planned to reveal his big secret. For a brief couple of hours, as they rode through the familiar lanes of Buckinghamshire, Mary Ann even shared in her husband's excitement. As the journey progressed, the landscape started to feel bigger. It was less homely, and more daunting. Eventually, they arrived in the wide open fields of Southall and Heston. The wide-eyed William helped Mary Ann from the cart, and holding her hand firmly, he escorted her out into the middle of the field. With each faltering step, Mary Ann felt the knot in her heart tighten. Oblivious, William picked up handfuls of soil and smeared it into his face, laughing at his own mischievous game. Mary Ann felt like she was in the company of a boy, younger even than her own sons.

"We are going to build Southall, my love. We are going to build this town, with homes and places where people can work. We are going to build something that will provide a better life for our children."

Mary Ann tried to hide an escaping tear. She knew that there was no going back, but that was precisely what she wanted to do. To jump onto the cart, and drive away from this nightmare, as fast as the nag would pull her. She hated her husband for taking her away from all that was dear to her. She hated herself for not being able to share William's joy. She also knew that once the children saw this new space, they would fall in love with its potential and she would be left quite alone. William pulled her close, to plant a kiss on her cheek, but she was repulsed by the soil on his face and all that it stood for. William let go of her hand, and started a playful dance by himself, across the field. It was at, that point, that Mary Ann could no longer conceal her tears, and she felt her heart starting to break. William didn't notice. He was talking enthusiastically to another happy young couple about the possibilities of building a pub on the very spot on which they stood.

"I think The Jolly Cricketers would be a most apt name for such an establishment."

Mary Ann Worley died in Hanwell Lunatic Asylum on 1st October 1879.

William Worley Junior and Mary Ann were the first Worleys to be connected with, and to settle in Southall. I grew up in the town that William helped build.

7. Fourteen

I became 14 years old in March 1973. My great-grandfather, James Neary, turned 14 in November 1848.

I can remember quite vividly my preoccupations as a fourteen-year-old. Would The Sweet be able to follow up their number one success with 'Blockbuster', with their next single, 'Hell Raiser'? Would Southall Football Club be able to hang on to the mercurial Alan Devonshire long enough to launch a concerted promotion push before he could be gobbled up by a professional team? Would I be taken on as a Saturday boy at Fine Fare, the Grocers? Would Auntie Hilda knit me another garish, nipple chafing tank top for my birthday?

The outcomes of those preoccupations were:

1. No.

Hell Raiser started an agonising run of form that saw The Sweet's next three singles stall frustratingly at number two. I met Steve Priest in 1974, although "met" might be a bit of an exaggeration. It was my first trip out after a nasty bout of chicken pox. I had popped into Hayes to buy, (surprise surprise), 'Teenage Rampage'. I was waiting at the bus stop to come home, when a chauffeur-driven Jaguar pulled up outside the café opposite. The driver got out, unfurled an umbrella and escorted Steve Priest inside for a Full English. I followed him in and from what was left of my pocket money, I purchased a warm Panda Cola. I'd like to report that I engaged Steve in a debate about great guitar riffs and the easiest way to apply mascara. I didn't. I was a demure little flower at fourteen.

2. Yes & No.

We held on to Alan Devonshire for our promotion season, sold him to West Ham and promptly got relegated. Such was life as a Southall supporter. Gordon Hill, Chris Hutchings and Les Ferdinand went exactly the same way; a fleeting moment of success whilst they were in our ranks, followed by season after season of crashing demotions after they left.

3. Yes.

It was the start of a wonderful four years of slicing luncheon meat with an egg in the middle and overcoming my distrust of the rollmop herring. The shop was run mainly by women with Alan Bennett names like Nellie, Marjorie, and Glad. Under the watchful eye of Mr. Ernest Tipper, I learned the ropes on the cooked meats counter and after a very brief apprenticeship, I was trusted to work the ham slicer. Mr Tipper used to boil the hams on the premises and that pungent smell stuck to my Levis for days.

I wasn't too enamoured of Marjorie. Every Saturday, before we opened, Marjorie would wait until Mr. Tipper was otherwise engaged and demand that I did her, "Half a pound of the scrag ends of ham and slip a couple of nice slices in the middle". It was fraud, pure and simple. The scrag ends sold for next to nothing, whilst Mr. Tipper's speciality hams were the most expensive item on the counter. One week, Marjorie came round and asked for her usual order to be upped to a whole pound of scrag ends with three slices of the best stuff thrown in the middle, because she was "entertaining Jim's manager from Wycombe for tea on Sunday". I flipped. She could have got me into serious bother. When she came to collect her order at closing time, she hadn't noticed that I had served up exactly what she had asked for, but I had also given her a bonus by slipping a rollmop herring in the middle. Explain that to Jim's manager.

4. Yes.

A purple/yellow/lime one. The upside was, that this one was only three sizes too small.

One hundred and twenty five years earlier, my great-grandfather, James Neary had also celebrated his 14th birthday. For the first thirteen years of his life, he had passed his birthday in Harrow High Street, at the grocers' shop where he lived with his parents and his three brothers. From about the age of eight, he had been expected to help out in his father's shop and most of his birthdays were marked by a celebratory tea of sausages and rollmop herrings; but only after he had worked his eight-hour shift. Working in the shop was not what made his young heart sing though. The tedium of the shop was only broken on Tuesday mornings. His father supplied the groceries for the nearby Harrow Public School and James enjoyed the opportunity to be outside, pulling the heavy cart up the hill to the school. If he was very lucky, he might even be rewarded with a penny tip from the lovely housekeeper. On his fourteenth birthday, however, James was many miles away from serving the housewives of Pinner or dragging the grocery cart up the Peterborough Road.

A few weeks before turning fourteen, James had enlisted in the Royal Navy. He remembered breaking the news to his family. His mother cried for three days and his father, quite literally, turned his back on him. They were never to speak again. Nobody came to see him off and he looked a forlorn figure as he begged travellers for a ride on their carts to Portsea. However, before the journey was half complete, James felt his mood lift and he realised that he now had the freedom to dream.

James Neary adjusted quickly and happily to his new surroundings aboard ship. Training, what there was of it, was on the job, so to speak, so he set sail on his first assignment within days of signing up. If there had been fourteen birthday candles to be extinguished, they would have been lit on board HMS Camus, early into its 102 day passage to China and the Navy's participation in the China opium wars.

The journey was long, tortuous and fraught with unexpe
danger. James had never seen waves in the water before ......
nothing in his imagination could have prepared him for
waves that were taller than the ship itself. In those very early
days of his naval career, James had the ranking of "Boy" in
the second regiment class. Most of the other boys hid in the
lower decks whenever mountainous waves loomed, but
James found them exhilarating and he truly understood the
meaning of being alive as viscous spray nearly washed him
overboard. He faced the birch on his third night at sea after an
officer found James with his shirt off, arms outstretched,
revelling in the waves on the poop deck. When James was
seven, the circus had came to Harrow and he had witnessed a
neighbour, who had volunteered to put his head inside a
tiger's mouth, being mauled to death by the creature. That
was danger, in James's eyes, not feeling the full force of an
Atlantic wave. He had not considered that exposing himself
to the elements might not only be endangering his own life,
but the lives of his fellows, by adding his jobs to their
workloads. Duty, in Her Majesty's services, James learned,
was the sternest of taskmasters.

James had never known pain like the birching. His back was
still bleeding, three days later. But not even the pain and
humiliation could quench James's fascination with and
admiration for the sixty-foot rollers. The officers observing
him might have believed that his subsequent caution was a
sign of a lesson having been learned. Inwardly, James smiled.
He had learned an important lesson, just not the one the

officers were expecting. He learned that you had to know how to play the game and he was grateful that the officers couldn't look inside him and see his dancing soul.

Being one of the youngest on the sloop, James' daily tasks were pretty menial and he spent much of his days as a powder monkey, cleaning and maintaining the gun deck with its small arsenal of eighteen guns. James was one of the fittest of the boys and enjoyed the challenge of carrying the gunpowder from the Hold to the artillery deck, several times a day. The other boys laughed at his eagerness for any task, but James knew that he was in the Navy for the long haul and was keen to learn everything there was to know about military duty.

James surprised himself with how quickly he adapted to the strict hierarchies aboard ship. Throughout his young life, James had never been a cap doffer. In the small world of Harrow, there was a lot of that subservience and James had carved out the reputation as a bit of a rebel. Whether it be his uncles or the respectable customers at the shop or the masters at Harrow school, James had a lazy temperament when it came to what he called;

"The Yes, Sir. No, Sir, Three bags full, Sir, poshies."

He quickly learned on the Camus that practically everyone he encountered expected a "Yes, Sir. No, Sir," when he spoke to them and for the first time ever, it didn't rankle.

There were many dark times during that first three-month journey. There were sporadic skirmishes with enemy ships and James quickly became accustomed to the sea burials of his friends and commanding officers. Men, who one day would be laughing and joking about the weevily biscuits, and then the next day, their ending was being marked with a prayer and a splash. Horrendous injuries to his colleagues became a daily pattern and James needed a strong stomach to tend to their wounds. James was frequently mocked or reminded that he was 'just a boy', but when the battles were heated, the ages of the crew became irrelevant. James, at fourteen, could have been as heroic, or as dead, as the ship's captain, thirty years his senior.

The night of his birthday, James would continue his work alone, standing watch on A deck. Everybody else, not on watch, had turned in for the evening, but James was in the habit of minding his business whilst staring into the vast, menacing expanse. He celebrated the man that he was becoming. He fancied that he could see Harrow on the distant horizon and a much older version of James Neary, in his blue apron, patting great slabs of butter into saleable shapes. He could see his father, getting older, but still greeting his customers with a cheery joke. He celebrated that arduous journey to Portsea where he had found a small package his mother had packed into his bag. The package contained some food from the shop and his grandmother's broach.

"Neary. Get to your hammock."

James obeyed for fear of another punishment, but he knew that he had exercised wisdom in choosing this life change. In just one month, the rolling sea had opened his eyes and the stars at night had opened his heart.

The only thing missing was someone who could say, "Happy birthday, James".

8. Jimmy Fontana

I have three records in my collection that have the name "Carol Worley" written on a sticky label, and stuck on the paper sleeve. Carol Worley is my Cousin. She is ten years older than me. Back in the day, when I was struggling to get the world to acknowledge my superior reggae dancing, Carol epitomised everything that was cool, to me. In the sixties, I had her pegged as a Sandie Shaw character. The jet black hair, the mini-skirts; I could easily imagine her singing barefoot on 'Top of the Pops'. She could possibly have been a modette, if I understood that cultural reference at my young age. We would often go and visit Carol's parents, Uncle Albert and Auntie Peg, for Sunday tea, but Carol was invariably absent. I had visions of her gadding about in Carnaby Street and having a banana longboat in a Wimpey, whilst I was stuck with dressed crab and melon balls in Hayes. Whatever she was doing, I always assumed that it was a damn sight more interesting than I was doing. It wasn't jealousy on my part; it was pure awe and admiration.

The three records were: 'In The Bad Bad Old Days' by The Foundations; 'Lady Willpower' by Gary Puckett and the Union Gap, and 'El Mundo' by Jimmy Fontana. Nearly fifty years on, those three dynamite pieces of vinyl still feature heavily in my Top One Hundred songs of all time. How they appeared in my record collection is hazy, but I probably nicked them at one of our family New Year's Eve parties that I used to look forward to each year. I invariably appointed myself as the disc jockey, and everyone would bring their favourite records along, to help the party go with a swing. Auntie Wilky would bring along her Englebert Humperdinck's and her Vince Hill's. Auntie Hilda would proudly offer her vast collection of Mrs Mills' long players. My contributions were more up to date and straight out of the hit parade, but no matter what latest trend I had bought into, Carol would always trump everyone for sublime cool.

In 1970, we went to a Pontin's holiday camp at Bracklesham Bay in Sussex. It was World Cup year, and all the happy campers had gathered in the ballroom to watch the Brazil vs. England big match. Geoff Hurst on the pitch and Brian Clough in the studio. The anticipation was huge. Back in the ballroom, it was all very polite, and the campers showed impeccable manners. There was no shouting and only occasionally some muted cheering. Definitely no swearing. We clapped politely when Gordon Banks made his incredible save from Pele. There was no rowdy behaviour when the final whistle blew, and England lost. We obligingly trooped off in a line to the pool, and assembled for the weekly beauty contest; the swimsuit round. Needless to say, my holiday song from 1970 was 'Back Home' by the England Football squad, and I am sure I would have made it my pick of my hit parade at the 1970 New Year's Eve party. "Come on, Uncle Bob. It's Back Home. Shake your tail feather."

By 1970, Uncle Albert and Auntie Peg had fully embraced the package holiday and took a fortnight in Majorca. Whilst I was hero worshipping Gary Puckett, Uncle Albert was lobbying for a knighthood for Freddie Laker. Looking at this time through 2020 eyes, it seems almost hideous, but we looked upon Uncle Albert and Auntie Peg as the total adventurers. I did a school project on Captain Cook, and I held Uncle Albert in similar esteem. The shine went off slightly after I watched 'Carry on Abroad' and was shocked to realise that places like Hotel Els Bells weren't quite as glamorous and sophisticated as Judith Chalmers had led us to believe. Despite my discovery that package holidays might not be all they've been cracked up to be, Carol scored several cool bonus points by returning home with 'El Mundo' by Jimmy Fontana. A massive continental hit from Majorca definitely outstripped 'Back Home', purchased from the Bracklesham Bay branch of Rumbelows.

I learned all the words to 'El Mundo'. If I had been brave enough, I would have performed it at the 1971 Pontins, Bracklesham Bay Junior Talent Contest. My Mum would have been as pleased as punch, if my outstanding vocal ability had won us a free, return holiday in September, to take part in the Grand Finals. Unfortunately, my vocal chords were weak, and my backbone was weaker still, so the Sussex holidaymakers were spared my Jimmy Fontana tribute act. The closest we ever came to winning a free September holiday was when Dad won the underwater swimming competition. Every spectator in the grandstand held their breath as Dad completed his winning, one length and three quarters. Unfortunately, Dad only got two weeks off work each year, so we had to decline the autumn invitation.

Although I was word perfect at *El Mundo*, I had no idea what the actual words meant. It was several decades later, and the introduction of Google translation, that I put the lyrics through the translating mincer. The words instantly lost all their appeal. I studied French for A Level, and the greatest appeal of French to me was the sound of the language. In Spanish, the sound of the lyrics sounded what I imagined beautiful, but dirty sex to sound like. El Mundo in its native tongue takes me floating high above the mountains, before dropping spectacularly into the crystal blue sea. It has me emerging from the sea, more swarthy than Daniel Craig, whilst scores of senoritas swoon at my knees. El Mundo, translated into English, conjures up images of Charles Hawtrey, lying pissed, on a sun lounger, at Pinewood.

El Mundo has helped me through life. It can disappear off my radar for years, but like a faithful Spanish el perro, it always returns. I have it on a loop on my Spotify, as I write this chapter. For me, it is part dreamy fantasy: and part Schoppenhaeur. It is beauty and ugliness. It is love and pain. As the chorus builds, I am transported back to my French A Level course and Voltaire's 'Candide'. Jimmy Fontana could be Doctor Pangloss delivering his final line, where he announces that he's seen all the horrors of the world, and now he's off to cultivate his own garden.

On the Costa del Sol, El Mundo is like inhaling exquisite pure air. On the front at Camber Sands, it's a bloody soppy song, strangled by its own winsome sentiment. How can you be part of a greater whole, whilst maintaining your own sense of self, is a question raised by El Mundo that can cause deep restlessness when you're an acne-ridden teenager. But it's sung with a Spanish swish that appeals to me as much as a man in his sixties, as it did to the eleven year-old me. The boy who was trying to match his cousin for cool, by apeing the vocal dynamics of Emlyn Hughes.

"El Mundo.
No se la parado ni un momento.
La noche le sigue al dia.
Y el dia vendra.

Esta noche amor, no he pensado mas.
En ti,
En ti."

The funny thing was that Uncle Albert, Auntie Peg and Carol were not the first members of the Worley family to travel to Spain, although they were probably the first Worleys to know all the words to the second verse of 'Y Viva Espana'.

It was one fine April morning in 1811 that Moses and Anne Paget dragged their cumbersome crates and battered trunks along the dockside at the Port of Barossa. What little money they had left after two weeks of bartering for stockings in the

Spanish markets, had to be spent sparingly. There was still the matter of the cost of sailing home to be negotiated, so a cart to carry the luggage was out of the question.

Moses looked at his wife with a mixture of pride, and not a little guilt. Three weeks away from her expected date of confinement, Anne displayed her customary pluck, and ignored the danger that carrying two heavy cases might pose for a woman in her condition. It was in the Spanish mercados that Anne truly came alive. Not for her, the drudgery of the life of a working class mother in England. To observe Anne, bartering loudly and with broad humour, was to see a woman, unafraid to mix in the rough, male world of stocking trading. Moses blessed his good fortune, in choosing his lifelong companion, so well.

Finally, the Pagets found their boat. They had already paid a large deposit for their passage, and Anne had been silently fretting that the captain of the boat had been no such thing and, like a scoundrel, had departed with their money. Her anxiety was unfounded as the ruddy faced skipper relieved her of her load, and offered his arm to help her board. No such assistance was offered to Moses who was left to hurl his own boxes onto the deck.

The captain's wife came out from her quarters, with a plentiful tray of bread and fruits. Within minutes of departing, the motley passengers were replenished and enjoying themselves with a raucous chorus of sea shanties.

Anne had her own bawdy repertoire which she bellowed out as the small boat ploughed its way through the ocean.

Moses, in utter contentment, stroked his wife's round belly, and waited expectantly for the scorching sun of the Gibraltar Straits..........

9. Louisa Paget

All throughout her life, Louisa Paget had been the source of other people's disbelief. The family that she married into, the Fleetwoods, would whisper their doubts behind Louisa's back. Nobody was brave enough to challenge the feisty Louisa to her face, but she knew what they were saying. And as far as she was concerned, they could all do a flying jump off London's tallest building. A formidable, successful business woman, Louisa refused to be cowed by the lack of imagination of those naysayers who couldn't begin to comprehend the type of world that Louisa was born into in 1811. More fool them, she often thought to herself. She knew where she came from and was proud of it. She remembered the story that her parents had told her many times and was keen that her vast family would learn about Louisa's first days in the world. It would take more than the raised eyebrow of a nuisance census taker, to dissuade her from her belief in her history.

It was early 1811 and Moses and Anne Paget were returning to England from an arduous, and frankly, unrewarding trip to Southern Europe. The journey had been meant to boost the trade that Moses and Anne had committed themselves to, since the early days of their marriage. Mr Paget knew that the trip had carried grave risks, not only financially. The passage had necessitated leaving his three small children with Anne's family for four months. There was also the additional hinderance of the imminent arrival of their fourth child and the inherent problems of a heavily pregnant woman taking part in such a hazardous sea passage.

Not that Anne Paget would have expected, or wanted mollycoddling. Both she and Moses Paget were fortunate to be instilled with a self-belief that saw mainly positives, in a fragile, unequal world. Moses was no Icarus however, and was acutely aware of the value his wife brought to the opening stages in a blossoming trading relationship. In other times, Anne Paget would have been lauded for her astute business brain. She was a numbers woman. Moses relied on his charisma and his admirable work ethic, but he was humble enough to acknowledge, privately that Anne was the power behind the throne. On a purely pragmatic level, if your trade is in silk stockings, the input of a wise woman, should not be dismissed.

And so it was, during the blistering hot, Mediterranean Spring of 1811, the Pagets found themselves on a commercial boat, along with sixty of their trading contemporaries, exhausted from their individual excursions, but relieved that their journey was on its last leg and home beckoned. Anne supressed a growing disquiet about the risk of so many passengers being packed like sardines onto such a small boat.

At this same time, the British Naval ship, HMS Warspite was stationed at the neck of the Strait of Gibraltar. For once, the crew were not centrally involved in any battles. Their presence in Gibraltar, amounted to nothing more than providing assistance to the Spanish and Portuguese fleets, as they tried to repel the invasion of the French Empire. It was a novel role for the officers and crew of the Warspite and, if truth be told, they were all silently relishing their supporting role in this bloodiest of conflicts. The Peninsular War was now in its

fourth year and the English bystander might have believed that the war's conclusion was as far away today, as it was the day hostilities started. Historians would later describe these hostilities as one of the first wars of large scale guerilla warfare, but from their position at the outside of the Strait, this analysis would have been lost on the English. To many of them, this mission was viewed as nothing more than an unexpected, extended holiday.

Rounding the bend, with the aim of entering the Gibraltar Strait, the small commercial boat, at first, missed the imposing French galleon that loomed menacingly, not many furlongs away. Moses and Anne Paget emerged from their afternoon slumbers, out onto the poop deck. They were both looking forward to dining well later, on the rich seafood that the men had caught that morning. The couple shared their plans for the future, revisiting their decision to move home to Wiltshire. Moses had heard good stories of this upcoming county and was feeling hopeful of the prosperity that Sherston Magna promised. As they shared an early evening rum, the Pagets felt satisfied that their decision had been a wise one and that they would soon be in an area of England that offered more opportunities of good fortune and health for their three children and the baby whose arrival was imminent.

BOOM.

The men on the French galleon decided upon some afternoon sport. The first cannon ripped through the side of the fishing boat and Anne was thrown immediately into the water. Fully dressed and a non-swimmer, she struggled to remain afloat. Moses had to act fast. He dragged the largest barrel that he could lay his hands on to the edge of the boat and using every sinew of strength that he could summon, he managed to push the barrel overboard. He prayed to God that his instinct was correct and that the receptacle would float. God was watching. Satisfied that the barrel would stay upright, Moses threw himself into the sea and swam with all his might towards Anne, who by this time, kept disappearing under the water. He couldn't have delayed a second longer. Another cannon was fired. Staring on in dismay from the sea, Moses saw the direct strike and before he could take in the full horror, the vessel which a few minutes earlier had been his passport home to England had overturned. He watched and listened in horror as severed limbs flew through the air and his newly acquainted fellow passengers screamed as they faced their doom.

Quickly, Moses remembered that he had work to do. He cradled his wife in one arm as he desperately tried to head back towards the bobbing barrel. He could do no more than a meagre paddle due to the power of the waves and the dead weight of his heavily pregnant wife. A man needs a miracle at times like these and by some amazing good fortune, a section of the disintegrating boat broke away from the main hull and landed directly in the Paget's path. Nowhere near big enough to act as a raft to be climbed upon, the debris at least floated and was wide enough for both Moses and Anne to grip on to. For the first time in several minutes, Moses allowed himself to breathe. He had no idea how long he would be able to keep hold of this tenuous liferaft and he became aware of the blood seeping through Anne's coat and realised that she had caught an injury through the blast. He also noticed that he was feeling light of head and feared that he may not be able to retain consciousness until any rescue might arrive. Anne started to sing and Moses felt that his heart might break.

 The Warspite moved towards the wreckage and as it did so, the French ship started to sail away from the scene of carnage that it had created. It's crew had no appetite for a fracas with the imposing warship. Well versed in sea rescues, the men on board the Warspite put years of experience into action and started to lower the cargo slings and ladders to aid the frightened survivors. Moses knew that it would be next to impossible, in her condition, for Anne to attempt the steep climb up a ladder, so dragged her across the water to the nearest haul. Knowing that saving her would probably lead to his own perishing, he put his last mortal energy into hoisting Anne into the haul. Having completed his task, Moses knew that Anne's fate and that of their child now rested in the hands of the naval crew and the good Lord.

Anne Paget awoke. She was in unfamiliar surroundings. Unfamiliar faces stared back at her, from her bedside. It took several minutes for Anne to rouse herself enough to collect her bearings. The first thing she noticed was that she wasn't in a bed, but laying on a mound of rags on a wretched damp floor. As she took in more of her surroundings, she became aware of a familiar sensation, down below.

A tall man, dressed in high ranking English naval uniform, stepped forward from the observing throng and took hold of Anne's hand.

"Do not distress yourself Madam. You took a formidable battering. You are being treated for your injuries on the English warship, Warspite. Your boat was attacked by Napoleon's ungallant peasants. We believe that only eleven people survived, although we have no idea how many passengers the boat was carr...."

"The baby. It's coming. NOW!"

"Madam. We have to observe certain formalities here. I have some questions...."

"Sod your formalities. I am about to give birth."

One of the young officers yielded to temptation and pulled back the blanket that was covering Anne. He turned as red as a beetroot.

"Sir. The lady is right. I think the head is starting to show…"

"Of course the head is starting to show. Now, if you can't be useful, sling yer hooks, the lot of you."

"Madam. Please stop interrupting. I am a senior officer on this ship. We must observe rank....."

Anne let out a noise that was later described as like a wolf being attacked by a bear. Most of the men instinctively took their leave.

"Look. I'll do this myself, but I don't want no sodding audience. You can stay though."

Anne was pointing at the inquisitive junior. He looked like he was about to faint. Knowing that the time for regular naval customs had long gone, the senior officer stepped backwards out of the door. Not before intuitively saluting the resourceful woman first. The last thing he heard was Anne's instruction:

"If you start pulling before I tell you to, I'll have your guts for garters….."

24 hours later.

Anne woke from a short, but peaceful sleep. Her new friend, First Officer Barnabus Tree, was fast asleep beside her. Anne collected her senses.

"Hello. Is there anybody there?"

Tree jumped to his feet and several other seamen bounded through the door.

"Where is my Moses? What happened to my husband?"

The senior officer stepped forward:

"Madam. Your husband survived. With narily a graze on him. He is helping my crew to clean the Hold, as a way of earning his passage back to England. I will ask one of my officers to bring him to you."

"And my child? It will need feeding. I'm guessing I'm the only person on this boat who can do that."

Barnabus took Anne's hand.

"Don't you worry, Madam. She's a bonny one is that little 'un. I tried to give her some brandy, but she…."

"Yes, thank you Tree. I'm sure Mrs Paget is very grateful for your…. Oh, here they are now.."

The crew parted, and through an almost ceremonial opening, Anne saw her beloved husband, Moses, walking towards her. He was carrying a small bundle, wrapped in the finest silk stockings. Barnabus Tree finally succumbed to his emotional state. A few men cheered. The tall, commanding officer patted his eye.

Over the next couple of days, the infant, Louisa Paget was declared the official ship's mascot. It was an honour that she would wear with pride.

Sixty-two years later, in 1873, a woman stood proudly in her newly opened tailor's shop. She surveyed the fruits of her long, successful career. She remembered how her blissful childhood in Wiltshire ended so abruptly on that fateful day when her father fell from the roof.

She remembered the abject poverty and the humiliation of those several spells in the workhouse with her proud mother and invalid father. She remembered her vow to never inflict the same shame on her children, if she should be so blessed. She remembered the early days of her marriage to the giant, Reuben, and how blasted history repeated itself and they were forced to throw themselves on the mercy of the Parish workhouse. From the workhouse, there followed many years of travelling the country, in search of work; from London to Ireland, and from Nottingham to Lancashire. It was only when they arrived in Brentford, that their luck started to change.

Louisa Paget's bosom swelled with pride. She was standing in the third, yes, the third tailor's and outfitters shop in Brentford that she and Reuben had opened over the past twenty years. Never truly satisfied with her lot, Louisa had ambitions that before long, Brentford High Street would be resplendent with a whole chain of Fleetwood stores. This latest one was managed by herself and her sturdy daughter-in-law, Emma. Abandoned by Louisa's feckless son, Reuben Junior and with five young children to raise, the fortitude of Emma was greatly admired by Louisa. And although, not a blood Fleetwood, Louisa held no qualms in entrusting this latest part of her empire to her reliable daughter-in-law.

Louisa settled her pride aside, satisfied that she had raised a family of shrewd survivors, in her own image.

Louisa Fleetwood/Paget allowed herself a throaty chuckle. It was a laugh that was familiar to all her family and customers, as was the story that Louisa had told, many times about how she had inherited such a deep, rasping laugh. She claimed, and nobody over a yard of ale would dare challenge her, that her vocal chords had been damaged by breathing in an excess of salty sea air in the first, four weeks of her life.

"Scoff all you like, my little dearios. What an introduction to this wonderful world."

10. The Lighterman

1873.

A tailors shop in Brentford. Louisa Fleetwood had locked up the premises for the day and retired to the nearby public house. As she stood and admired the fruits of several decade's labours, she failed to notice the five year old boy, lurking in the shadows of the gentlemen's overcoats. Once she had left, and with the shop to himself, the boy emerged from the shadows.

He loved this shop. He liked to smell the freshly pressed gowns. He enjoyed touching the cold, soft silks. He was fascinated by the elaborate stitching of the heavy capes. It reminded him of the many hours he had spent with his mother and grandmother, watching them attentively, as they painstakingly taught him this intricate skill. His grandmother had a most flamboyant style as she sewed. It was a talent that had been passed down, through several generations of his family. He was a boy, rich in imagination and he amused himself by standing on a crate behind the deep mahogany counters. He pretended to courteously serve the passing Dukes and Duchesses, who held his grandparent's wares in such high regard.

He seldom gave his father's absence a moment's thought. In spite of the considerable worldly knowledge he had amassed in his five years, he remained confused about his family's relationship with his father. He would disappear for months at a time, but his eventual returns to Brentford were always received like the welcome homecoming of a war hero. And yet, the boy knew that his father had not been absent in the course of war action. The family would gather in The Brewery Tap and listen with good humour, as his father took centre stage and recounted his latest adventures. His grandmother, especially, would consume too much ale and slap her thigh vigorously as his father told his latest tall tale. But the boy wasn't taken in. Although he hadn't yet achieved the wisdom to be able to name it, he was aware of a knot of resentment that would tighten, as his father launched into another fantastical story. The boy got into the habit of slipping out of the back of the public house and watched in awe as the boatman jostled for a clear position along the River Thames. The boy was unable to read as yet, but had a strong memory and would mentally catalogue each vessel, according to the the striking combinations of colours of the boats. Once seen, he never forgot any of the boats and he could retrieve any barge from his mental log at a moment's notice. Alongside the colours, the boy would register the state of disrepair of each boat and these features would be added to his formidable taxonomy.

The boy already had the unfocused seeds of a plan, growing in his head. An ancient lighterman by the name of Findlay would regularly wave to the boy whenever he sat in the yard of The Brewery Tap. In the boy's mind, Findlay must have been at least one hundred years old. His face was battered by a hundred year's worth of working in all weathers and raw sewage. However, Findlay's arms retained their youth and the boy had never seen a thicker, stronger pair of arms. They looked as solid, and as wide as the chestnut tree on the Green at the top of the High Street. The boy knew that, one day soon, he would find the courage to leave his position on the yard wall, head down to the riverbank and strike up a conversation with the ancient lighterman. Perhaps the next time that his father visited and the family would be distracted for several hours, the boy could make his escape. He laughed to himself because he knew, with all his heart, that he had the disposition to make this idea come true.

The boy left his position on the crate and said his farewells to the imaginary duchesses. He stood in the centre of the shop with his arms stretched wide. As the eldest son, he was heir apparent to this tailoring kingdom and he was starting to feel pride in this responsibility. Two years earlier, he had been summoned to his grandfather's deathbed and he remembered the gravity of being placed on his grandfather's lap, as all the adults assembled around the bed. As he grew in years, the boy recognised the significance of this event. It was the beginning of the succession. A communication to the other sons and daughters, where the future laid. The boy felt pride that day and he felt pride this day. And there was something else, that the boy was unable to distinguish. He skipped to the double window, at the front of the shop. He saw a busy High Street, with ladies shopping, the elegant coachmen going about their business and children playing. And in the distance, he saw the purple and orange of the Majestic Mary, moored for all eternity. If the boy had been able to identify that something else, he might have been shocked to know that it was restlessness.

1881.

A tailors shop in Brentford. 13 year-old Thomas Fleetwood stood in boredom at the worn mahogany counter. He had been standing in exactly the same position for an hour and he hadn't seen a single customer. It was Saturday morning and outside, the High Street was as busy as ever. But not in the shop. Thomas longed for the moment when the church clock struck one o'clock and his Aunt Eliza would arrive to relieve him of his interminable duty. The smells of the shop had long since, ceased to excite him. Now, there was only one smell that invaded every corner of this cell - the stench of death. The death of his grandmother Louisa, three years ago, started the decline of the shop. The death of his father, two months ago, was followed by the grotesque pantomime of Reuben Fleetwood Junior being laid out in his coffin, in the middle of the shop floor, for three days. Laying in State, was how the idiot aunts described the spectacle.

Thomas's mother was another cause of his disquiet. Giving birth to her sixth, surviving child, just seven weeks before his father's death, had given his mother a clear invitation to neglect her duties within the shop. Aunts, and uncles, and cousins, came and went, but none of them seemed to share any enthusiasm for the business that his grandmother had given her life to. They may have had enthusiasm for the shop's takings, but as the stock dwindled, so did the shop's reputation. The other thing that was seriously dwindling was Thomas's commitment to restoring Fleetwood's to its former glory.

At twenty five minutes past one, Thomas had changed out of his formal work clothes and was running expectantly towards the river. This was his first visit to the river since his father's wake, and he had an unfamiliar uncertainty about him. Trapped within the prison of the shop for over eight weeks, Thomas fretted that he had forgotten everything he had learned over the past seven years. Trying in vain to remember even the most basic of skills, he became even more frit. Solidly built for his thirteen years, he even imagined that he had lost a considerable amount of strength, during the official period of mourning. He had half a mind to turn turtle and return to the tailors. His mother would have been delighted, and his aunt would have been off like a whippet to join the rest of the family in the alehouse. "Keep going, Thomas. Keep going." In the distance, he could see Findlay working hard on the deck. Thomas kept going.

Thomas was keen to set to work, but Findlay was in the mood for some lunch. He offered Thomas some bread and some ale, and together they sat in silence, save for the noise of the pigeons who had suddenly appeared in the expectation of some crusts. They had chosen the wrong barge. Thomas was ravenous and he had never seen Findlay waste a morsel, in the course of their acquaintance.

"Sorry to hear about your Pa."

Thomas nodded. He didn't want to talk about his father. The minute that he had just set foot on the boat, a preposterous idea had occurred to him. Sweating with the excitement of his idea, he wondered how, or whether, he would be able to put the idea into words. Thomas needed help, but Findlay's next utterance proved that he would have to be very courageous.

"Expect you've been proper busy in the shop? Great responsibility on your shoulders now, lad."

Thomas could feel a lump in his throat. He got up and walked to the stern of the boat. For a brief moment, he wondered if he had gone deaf. The traffic on the river was as boisterous as ever, but all Thomas could hear was silence. He couldn't understand the evidence of his own eyes because the only vessel he could see out on the water was a solitary warship, docked on the opposite bank. A man and a woman waved to him and through squinted eyes, Thomas could see that the man was carrying a small baby. For a moment, Thomas suspected that there had been something untoward in his ale, because he would have sworn on the bible that the baby was his grandmother, Louisa. Thomas remembered the family stories about his grandmother having been born on a warship, but this was the makings of lunacy.

Thomas's musings were cut short by a loud splash and a chorus of effing and jeffing. Three familiar lightermen, all wretchedly drunk, were trying to drag a fourth man from the brown, muddy water. After a few minutes in which Findlay had joined in the rescue, the man was pulled out, onto the bank and he immediately started at fisticuffs with his three rescuers.

"Chuck him back in," laughed Findlay, as he reboarded his barge.

All his fears evaporated and Thomas leapt across the boat, grabbing Findlay by his arm.

"Findlay. I want to start my apprenticeship straightaway. Tomorrow. Please, Findlay. I have never been more certain of anything in my life."

"But what about the tailors shop, Boy? Your mother will be expecting big things from you. You've got duties."

"I'm not a tailor. I never have been and I never will be."

Thomas looked back across the Thames, but the warship had disappeared whilst he had been watching the fracas.

"Please, Findlay. I was meant to be on the water. That is in my blood too."

Findlay looked angry. In fact, he looked very angry. Thomas continued his pleading.

"If I'm going to start my apprenticeship to become a lighterman, I can think of no better teacher than you."

Findlay threw a loading crate into the water. Thomas became fearful that he may try to flog him. Findlay finished off the last of his ale, in one swallow. He looked at Thomas, and Thomas thought that he detected a wry smile.

"Tomorrow morning. 7 o'clock. Be late, and that's the end of my time."

Findlay strode off the boat and into the public house. Thomas fished the crate from the water, dried it off and sat down on it. He remained deep in concentration, until his thoughts were interrupted by the warm rain. He smiled a deep smile to himself.

"I had better finish off the rest of this ale before I break the news to Mother that I am now a lighterman."

1900.

It was late afternoon in a comfortable riverside cottage in Brentford. Mary Fleetwood was having a little sit down, after preparing the stew for this evening's supper. Her precious daughter, Emma, had not long come home from school and was entertaining herself, making some jewellery out of some tin that her father had collected from work.

Mary had a lot to occupy her thoughts. Earlier that afternoon, her brother Henry had paid a surprise visit. Against her better judgment, Mary held a true affection for her brother. He could be the complete rogue, but as everyone knew, his charm and humour had got him out of many scrapes. This was the second time that Henry had visited in as many weeks; a rarity, but a sign of his persistence whenever he got a bee in his bonnet. For the second time, Henry had made his proposal that was so ridiculous, so impossible that Mary wanted to laugh him out onto the street. But she hadn't, because something had been stirred. For the past few years, Henry had been doing some work for an American, a Mr Vanderbilt. Henry's tales often had to be taken with a pinch of salt, but this one appeared to be true. The story went that Mr Alfred Vanderbilt was one of the richest men in America and Henry first encountered him when the American visited England, with the intention of initiating the London to Brighton coach rallies. Mary couldn't deny that her brother was an expert horseman and groom, and it seemed that Mr Vanderbilt recognised the value of Henry's knowledge and took him on the payroll. Henry had already visited America twice and now, Mr Vanderbilt was offering to fund the whole

Daubney family to relocate to New York. Henry was not a man to take no for an answer and Mary could feel her resistance to the plan, weakening. Henry left her with the firm ultimatum that she had to come to a decision by the weekend. The ship to Ellis Island sails a fortnight, today.

How could Mary broach the subject with Thomas? She was absolutely sure that he would say "no", but her greatest fear was that he might say "yes". Despite the interference from his family, they had a good marriage and Mary was not sufficiently henpecked that she had to defer all the major decisions to him. Yet, just this once, she wished that that was the case because she couldn't bear the burden of being party to such a life-changing decision..

They had a good life together. Mary wished that they had been blessed with more children, but Emma was a good girl, and the apple of her father's eye. Thomas was an excellent provider and they never went without. He had proved the doubting Fleetwoods wrong and his decision to take to the water as a lighterman had long since been vindicated.

After the death of old Findlay in 1895, Thomas had taken sole ownership of the barge and brought in the kind of business that Findlay would never have imagined possible. Thomas was well trusted and his reliability, and adeptness on the water, was well recognised by the many traders who sought him out whenever their commerce brought them to London. Just in the last year, he had taken on three lightermen apprentices from the workhouse and he had confided in Mary that once the three boys achieved their licenses, Thomas fully intended to purchase a second barge. "If my grandparents could build up three tailors' shops in ten years, there is no reason why I cannot achieve three boats in the same time." And Mary knew that Thomas would make good of his word.

What perturbed Mary was that Thomas was now thirty-two. He had been working on the river for the best part of twenty years. He had expressed no desire for change, quite the contrary, but a man can become restless, especially when presented with new opportunities. Mary knew little of America, but Henry's accounts had painted a picture of America, where everything was bigger than England. She imagined bigger rivers, with bigger boats. Bigger pay packets to buy bigger homes. She knew that it would be hard for Thomas to refuse such adventure.

Mary's thoughts were interrupted by a loud knock on the door. Emma dashed into the room, but her mother was already in the hall. Emma took the lid off the stewing pan and sniffed the pungent aroma. She was hungry. Disconcerted, she thought that she heard a scream from the hall, followed by the sound of something heavy being dropped.

Suddenly, the parlour door opened and a man entered, carrying Mary in his arms. Frozen in fear, Emma relaxed as she recognised the man who she had seen playing cards with her father in the yard of The Brewery Tap.

"Don't be afraid, Emma. My name is Walter. Your mother has had a terrible shock."

At this point, Mary regained consciousness. She looked deathly pale and as if, she might collapse again. She seemed to have forgotten that Emma was in the room.

"How, Wally? How could he have drowned?"

"We don't know for sure, pet. There's been some boats, down all week from the North. Muscling in. No respect for us men who have been working the river, for years. They were getting Tommy's gander up. Anyway, this morning, Tommy and a couple of the other lightermen decided to row out and have it out with them....:

Both Mary and Walter appeared startled to suddenly hear Emma's voice.

"Mummy. Has something happened to Daddy?"

Mary took Emma in her arms.

"I'm afraid so, darling. Daddy has had a horrid accident. Please, Wally. Do go on."

"Well, that's about as much as we know, for sure. Our men tried to talk to their men, who thought it was all a joke. I could see Tommy rowing back, in a rare old temper. Cussing and kicking the side of his boat. And when I looked back again, he was gone. His boat was empty. Two of the lads dived in, but the tide made it treacherous and they had to stop. They thought the world of your Tommy, giving them a job. They're proper broken up about it. Anyways, his body washed up, not an hour since. I'm so very sorry, Mary."

That was that. Mary thought that her heart would stay broken forever. Emma disappeared into herself. Of course, America was now out of the question. What would people say? And there was an inquest to be had. Mary knew that her place was in Brentford.

Findings of an inquest held on 1st March 1900:

Thomas Fleetwood, aged 31 and a lighterman from 35 Grosvenor Road, Brentford, died at Brentford Docks on 26th February 1900.

The cause of death: Accidental drowning.

11. Buying A Suit

My history of buying a suit got off to a pretty inauspicious start. In fact, I'm still dealing with the scars of the event, 43 years later. I was due to start work at Nat West Bank on 16th August 1977 (which coincided with Elvis dying) and Uncle Albert promised me that he would buy me my first proper suit for the occasion. I turned up that morning in Hayes town, dressed as I was most days during that long hot summer: an Adidas t-shirt, jeans and a pair of trainers. All topped off with a pair of mirrored sunglasses, a fashion concept that Tom Cruise shamelessly stole from me, many years later. As I got off the bus and spotted Uncle Albert and Carol, who had come along for moral support, I instantly knew that I had made some terrible mistake. In the middle of Hayes High Street, Uncle Albert gave me the most demoralising bollocking. The humiliation was twofold. Not only did my dressing down take place so publicly, but the nature of it, revealed to me that I hadn't the first clue about the very adult and responsible task of buying a suit. Nobody had told me that to be fitted correctly for a suit, one had to wear a collar and tie, and a sensible pair of shoes. We marched into the outfitters and Uncle Albert conveyed in no uncertain terms his apologies that he was accompanying a social novice on this vitally important task.

My ego was round my ankles and I lost all interest in buying the suit. I must have tried on at least half a dozen different styles and eventually, Carol decided that the crocodile green, three-piece was the best fit. So, that was what I wore to work on the day that Elvis took his last shit on the toilet. I didn't want to work in a bank, but I had no idea what else I could do. It didn't need Mr Price to tell me, two years later that I was a square peg in a round hole; I knew that all too well. All the other male bank clerks had suits of grey or brown. I was the only bank teller in crocodile green.

Within eighteen months, I had become a mod and from that point on, all my suits have been two-tone ones. Apart from my wedding. I foolishly brought a heavy woollen, three-piece blue suit that was totally inappropriate for a baking hot 4th July. I was drenched in sweat before I even entered the registry office. Guests were worried that I was "going down with something". It was the same day as the famous five-set Wimbledon final between Borg and McEnroe and by the time I came to say "I do", I was perspiring as heavily as Mr McEnroe in the fifth set. I expect Borg had time for a shower before he kicked off the winners gala's waltz with Martina Navratilova, but Julie had to put up with a sweaty woolly man, dragging her around the dance floor to Heatwave's 'Always and Forever.'

That's all I've got to say about my 43 year history of suit buying. In 2019, I received my lump sum pension and decided that I needed a 'sensible suit.' One that wouldn't be out of place at a funeral, a bar mitzvah or at a talk to a room full of psychiatrists, waiting with unabated breath for me to tell the Get Steven Home story. With my pension burning a hole in my pocket, I decided to push the boat out and buy a made to measure suit. Uncle Albert would have been so proud of me.

I googled all the local tailors and settled on a company called 'Fleetwoods'. A chap popped round twice to measure me up and I settled back and waited for the final work of art to be delivered. A few weeks later, Steven came to find me in the kitchen and announced:

"Dad. There's a lady on the path, with a bike."

I went outside and there was a woman, who for all the world, was the spitting image of Miss Almira Gulch from The Wizard of Oz. Only, she was so tiny, she could have been a munchkin, just as easily. She was dressed from head to toe in black lace and had the most startling array of brightly coloured rings on each finger. She was riding a bicycle with a trailer behind, emblazoned with gaudy red lettering that spelled out "Fleetwoods Tailors." As she saw me open the front door, she waved most theatrically and parked her bike by next door's gate.

"Hello, my deerio. Lovely day for a beautiful new suit. I'm going to make you look a million dollars."

She let out the deepest cackle I had ever heard, causing Steven to rush back indoors and hide in his bedroom. I showed her into my bedroom so that we could proceed with the fitting and disconcertingly, she started to remove my cardigan whilst we were still walking down the hall. It had alarming shades of an over-eager call girl from a Robin Asquith movie. Within seconds, I was down to my underpants and whilst she put on a flamboyant show of dressing me in my new suit, she whistled a melody that would have made a cat howl. I loved her.

I loved the suit too. It was a lightweight number, but it had a timeless quality to it. It wouldn't raise any eyebrows at the psychiatrist's conference; neither would it have looked out of place at the annual Brentford tailors' balls of the 1850s. It fitted in all the right places and if I say so myself, I looked like the bees knees. Miss Gulch expanded with pride.

"Was you thinking of giving me a little tip, dear?"

"I was actually."

"I was wondering whether you might like to tip me with some ale. I passed a lovely little public house at the top of your road."

Who could resist such an offer?

"I can do better than that, Louisa. I'll throw in a bag of pork scratchings as well."

She grabbed my head in her hands, grazing my cheek on one of her rings as she did so and planted a huge smacker on my face.

"That's just the kind of tip, I's like."

And then she let out another ear-piercing cackle that made Steven dive under his bed for cover. I decided to change out of my new suit. It was too nice to make its debut at the Packet Boat Inn. I threw on something more suitable. Louisa checked out the stitching of my waistband and tutted loudly.

"This wouldn't have seen the light of day, back in my day," she remonstrated.

Fifteen minutes later, we were seated in the pub, me with a Guinness and Louisa with a triple brandy. All the stories that I had heard were true; she loved an audience. She flirted outrageously with the students from Brunel and even persuaded the old chap with his dog, to share half his bacon sandwich with her. I was secretly thankful that there wasn't a piano because I knew that she would want to give Cowley one of her sea shanties. That reminded me of the picture that I had downloaded a few weeks ago.

"I've got something that I think might interest you."

I got out my phone and scrolled through the photo albums. Eventually, I found the picture of the Warspite, looking majestic and towering over all the other ships and boats in the snap.

I hadn't bargained for Louisa's response though. She wept buckets. Loudly. Of course, it never occurred to me that she had never seen a picture of the vessel that she had been born on and that had been a major part of her anecdotal performances for many years.

"Oh, you little diamond. That's worth every suit in my shop. And more. To think that I'm holding a picture of the very ship that old Louisa Fleetwood first step foot into this world on."

More tears. One of the students came back from the toilet with a full roll for her. Her nose blowing was as garrulous as her laughter.

"This has made me day. I might need another brandy to calm me nerves," she sobbed, as she passed me her glass.

A few more triples later and my great-great-great grandmother was in full sail. I was struggling to find my land-legs too, but she was a hoot. I asked her about her time in the workhouse.

"Oh, the shame. There were some right sorts in there. Never the type of place for a respectable woman like me."

"How did you come to be in there? If I remember rightly, you'd been travelling backwards and forth between Ireland and the Midlands?"

"I wanted to settle. And if you were going to make any sort of money, it had to be London. My father had always dreamed of a shop, but then his accident put paid to that. We just couldn't get the money to get started."

"How did you get that first shop?"

"That part of the story is only for respectable company, my derrio."

"Go on. You can tell me....."

"We used to go down the river most days for our lunch. Take some bread and some fruit and a little drop of what you fancy. We'd passed that shop for years on our daily trip. Then, one day we heard that she'd died. The owner. So, I said to Reuben, 'we're moving in, old sweet,' and we did. He broke a window round the back and gave me a leg-up, and there we stayed."

"Squatting?"

"Seizing the moment, my Reuben called it. We were lucky. No buggar noticed for months, and by the time that they did, we'd earned a tasty little nest egg to put a deposit on the place."

"And never looked back?"

"Never looked back. No bloody point in looking back. That's not going to put food on the table and pins in your mouth, is it?"

The elderly chap with the dog bid his farewells after putting another triple brandy down before Louisa. She gave him a massive kiss on his cheek and planted another one on the dog. She was back in the moment. The workhouse and the first shop had left the Packet Boat in the same way as the man and his dog. I wanted to her ask her about her son, Reuben junior. He was Thomas Fleetwood's father and I knew nothing about him. He was the Scarlet Pimpernel. He was never around. He popped up enough to sire eight children, but didn't seem to play any part in their lives. I couldn't find any connection between him and the tailors shop. My instinct though was not to ask. Louisa was having a great day. I didn't want to spoil it. Besides, she was as soused as a herring and I didn't think that I was going to get much more sense out of her.

My day with Louisa ended with me wheeling her back to my flat. She was in no fit state to cycle all the way back to Brentford. She was already asleep on the bike and it was a real struggle to steer the thing and keep her from falling off at the same time.

I made a mental note to print off a copy of the Warspite.

12. Twenty

1979

The Railway Tavern, Southall. Me, Murphy and Jaz are in with the in crowd.

"Found myself in a strange town.

Though I've only been here for three weeks now.

I've got blisters on my feet.

Trying to find a friend in Oxford Street."

It's Paul Weller, man. The sixth lager. It's sweaty. Jaz has been caning the blues and announces that he's going to dive off the roof of the Kings Hall. He's been into Bruce Lee for over a year. Immortality is for pussies. I'm looking at Murphy. Murphy is due a slap. I've been scrutinising his Parka and he's amassed two more badges than me. Murphy is telling Jaz that we've got his back. If the Hamboro Tavern crew turn up, we've got his back. I agree that we've got his back, but I don't want any shit to go down before Margate. I'm no Bruce Lee. I like to think that I'm Jimmy from Quadrophenia. Paul Weller is getting louder. Jaz is telling us that he's going to do it, guys. We start chanting that Jaz is a flying machine.

Paul Weller stops. Bernie, the landlord, yells out, "Haven't you lot got any fucking homes to go to?" He rings the bell. We all jeer. Frank Wilson blasts out of the jukebox. We all cheer.

"Do I love you?

Do I love you?

Indeed, I do."

Murphy and I go the gents to polish off the last of his goodies bag. Frank Wilson is a heaven sent angel. I want to be Frank Wilson. Last night, I wanted to be Jackie Wilson. Murphy has got his arm around my shoulder and telling everyone that I am his best mate, as God is his witness. "Do I love you, Marky Mark? Indeed, I do." I piss myself, literally, with laughter. Murphy is doing his little cool dance and looks like a fucking superstar. I try to copy him, but I ain't got the moves. Bernie picks up a snooker cue. He wants his bed. The amateur. Murphy grabs the hood on my Parka. "Where's Jaz gone?" We leg it outside. Yelling his name. We both look up and scan the roof of the Kings Hall. Nowhere. Nobody. Murphy is shouting that we need to phone the Old Bill. Mrs Sidhu pulls up in her car. Jaz, smiling like a bastard, gets in. "See you two in Margate, my little grasshoppers." We rag him about needing his mother to take him home. Mrs Sidhu smiles, nervously. We've only got one mother between the three of us. Murphy and I haven't got a mother anymore. Frank Wilson has stopped. Indeed he has. We try to get back in the pub. Bernie has locked the door. The lightweight.

Three months later.

August bank holiday weekend. The only positive thing about being a bank clerk, which I am, is that the bank holiday was invented for us. I've been getting everything sorted for Margate since that night at the Railway. New tassels ? Tick. A pair of blue/grey two tone sta-press? Tick. A haircut by Alessandro? Tick. It's going to be ace. All the faces will be there. I'm not quite a face, but I'm moving up the ranks. Need to be alert to doing something eye catching in Margate. I'm not too keen on the violence. For me, this weekend is about the music and the clothes. And being seen. And being part of this fucking awesome Mod family. Jaz has only gone and got himself a scooter. That's what comes when both your parents are maths teachers. He will be one of the faces. Bruce Lee on a Lambretta. Me and Murphy will be getting the train. Murphy has got a pocketful of entertainment and the plan is that we'll be racing, before we even set foot on the front. I've done a compilation tape for the journey. I'm going to fill our compartment with some Iain Page. Here we go, Faces. Time for some action.

3pm. Bank holiday Sunday. I'm pacing the hospital corridor. I'm travelling too fast to sit down like all the other worried people in the waiting room. Murphy has gone outside for a fag. I need to keep my eye out for him. My lovely, quiet, charismatic Irish friend is after blood. Five minutes earlier, he was screaming in my face, "They didn't go for him because he was a Mod. They went for him because he's black." He was right. We hadn't seen a single Rocker since we arrived, yesterday. The word hadn't got out that the West London Mods would be in Margate. Catching the BBC News in the Radio Rentals window, it was clear that all the Faces had gone to Brighton. Then, the Rockers pitched up. In Brighton. An absolute bloodbath. Secretly, I was relieved, but joined in with the others, mocking the Rockers for going yellow belly on some Margate action. I was relieved, because without the violence, it left the weekend for the music, and the pills, and the laughs. I would have expected Murphy to see it the same way, but he was on a short fuse. One of his best mates had just been lamped.

Last night, we slept on the beach. We set up a two hour rota, so that one of us would be awake and spot if we were being washed out to sea. Or if any trouble might creep up on us whilst we were kipping. I woke up this morning, frozen to the marrow and soaking wet. The tide had started to come in. Murphy informed me that Jaz had gone off to get some bacon sandwiches, so we passed the time, arguing who was the best singer: Steve Ellis or Steve Marriott? I didn't know much about bliss, but if it exists, this must be what bliss feels like. Frankie Valli came on the compilation tape, singing, "The night begins to turn your head around." I couldn't make my feet behave. I'd been practising Murphy's cool dance moves and by the time of the second verse, we were both giving it large, in the sea. For three minutes and twenty seconds, Murphy and I were the faces. We got a round of applause. Jaz returned. Blood everywhere. This was our kung-fu king, but he'd been jumped by half a dozen locals, as he came out of the cafe. He tried to laugh it off, bragging how the scabby locals are looking worse than him, but he kept drifting away. An old fella, walking his dog, told us that he'd fetch his car and drive us to the hospital.

Two days later. The first day back at work since Margate. I was printing cheque books and my ear was sore. Jaz was fine. Heavily bandaged, ego bruised, but fine. Four knife cuts to his body. That'll increase his status, no end. Murphy drove Jaz's scooter back to Southall, whilst I became Jaz's nurse cum bodyguard on the train. Phil Daniels would have gone back, but I was knackered. All I wanted to do was sleep and rehydrate.

That afternoon, I was called into the manager's office. Apparently, one of the customers had complained about my earring. The three of us had our ears pierced in Margate in a Three Musketeers type of gesture. Mr Price told me that if I didn't take the earring out immediately, he would have to consider my position. He went on to say that, thinking about it, moving on, might be the best thing for me. The last thing he said as I walked backwards, out of the room was, "Let's face it, Neary. With you, we've been trying to fit a square peg, into a round hole." He meant it as an insult, but it was the best compliment I could have received. I didn't want to be in a fucking round hole. I had to play it sweet, though. I had already been interviewed for a new job in the civil service and didn't want to screw up my reference. Sometimes in playing the long game, a face has to play it neat.

To get the stench of Mr Price's appalling bad breath out of my nostrils, I went to Southall market and brought myself a pork pie hat, and a copy of 'Interloop' by The Tymes.

1855.

Port Royal, Jamaica. The second master of HMS Castor, twenty year-old James Neary, was waking up after the night before; and what a swell night it had been. James turned over in the bed. Sleeping next to him was Genevieve, his favourite girl from Mistress Sophia's house. She stirred and smiled at him. James reached for her, but she swatted at his hands.

"What?" he said. "I paid for a whole night."

"It's morning now."

"It's not time for me to leave."

James reached for his lambskin sheath and his little bottle of neatsfoot oil. Many of his crew were presently being treated for syphilis. In fact, the fatalities from this foul affliction during his six years of service had been shockingly high. Unlike several of his older shipmates, James wasn't encumbered with having to send the majority of his earnings back home to England to support a family, so besides companionship, he could afford protection, as recommended by the Master's mate who had taken the fifteen-year-old James for his first encounter in a brothel.

"Wrap up warm, as yer Mum would have said," had been his advice. "When you're goin' down a well-trodden path, it's bound to be muddy, so make sure you keeps yer boots on, if you catch me drift." James had indeed caught his drift, invested several weeks' wages in a different kind of footwear and as a result, hadn't caught anything unpleasant. He oiled the sheath, dry after its rinsing the night before. Then he turned to Genevieve and plied his still-slippery fingers to overcome her token resistance.

Afterwards, James lay back in a pleasant glow. The girl rose to wash, and he gently slapped her rounded rump.

"Get me some breakfast."

She shot him a look that held a warning. "I'm not your housegirl."

"C'mon, you know I'll pay you and you know that I'm a special guest."

She paused, nodded.

"Extra tip, and I'll even say please. Please, beautiful, generous Genevieve." He caught her hand and pressed his lips to the back of it.

Her lips tilted upwards again.

"You not a stingy one, and you are a pretty talker, that's a fact."

Tying her wrapper around her, she opened the shutters then left the room. James put her pillow on top of his, settled luxuriously with his hands behind his head and let his thoughts wander, as he gazed out over the town towards the sea.

Port Royal had a chequered history. In the mid to late seventeenth century, the island had been booming as an unlikely centre for much of the world's trade. The island was also a Mecca for piracy and had earned itself the dubious, but catchy, title of, 'The sin capital of the world'. Every third building was a drinking palace and every street had at least one whorehouse. Then, in 1692, an earthquake struck and a third of the island disappeared into the sea forever. Of the surviving population, two-thirds were dead by the end of the year, from typhoid or other diseases, caused by the aftermath of the earthquake.

By the time of James Neary's arrival in 1855, the island of Port Royal had stabilised to a large extent. The British government publicly promoted the island as having left its debauched history behind, and being now a haven of legitimate trade in a place of God-fearing, Christian values. In private, they had less noble aims.

This was the landscape in which James Neary had celebrated his twentieth birthday. Rank and seniority had necessitated a certain distance between James and his men when it came to social gallivanting. James hadn't yet held his rank long enough to be fully accepted into the Masters' club, which played by different rules from those of the lower orders. It could have led to a rather lonely celebration, but James was well-respected by the small crew under his command. Any indiscretion on James's part would have been tolerated, covered, and even admired by his loyal men. And so it was that on 30th November 1855, James Neary, with six of his crew and two newly enlisted Boys, could be found with full pockets and the firm intention of having a bountiful night ashore, in a small gin palace, far enough away from the main port to avoid unwelcome eyes.

The majority of the island's slaves had been freed at the beginning of the century. Most of them had moved to the mainland, but several of the more hardy souls had stayed and by 1855, ran most of Port Royal's drinking dens. James had spent many a night playing cards with one of the oldest ex-slaves, Victor, and a solid friendship had grown. James had been fascinated and in admiration of Victor's stories of his fight for freedom, while Victor had been amused to observe that whilst James was perfectly adept at life at sea within the strict confines of ship hierarchies, he could be all at sea when it came to navigating some of the trickier aspects of life on dry land. Victor had first encountered James on the naval officer's fourth day on the island. James had been instructed to go ashore and collect some supplies for the ship. Purchases collected, James took refuge from the scorching temperatures with a thirst-quenching tincture in Victor's drinking den. Two hours, and several rums later, James was out for the count. Three sailors who had been dispatched to find the missing seaman, carried the legless James back to the ship for the inevitable lashing. The supplies were forgotten about and later that evening, Victor took them to the Castor, with a tall story of how James had been set upon by some local rogues who were after his money and having seen them off, James had chanced upon the gin house for some necessary restoration. The story did not spare James a flogging, but that was not Victor's plan. Aware that the competition locally for the seamen's trade was keen, Victor knew that his charade would curry favour amongst the sailors, looking for a safe place for their inebriation. The next time that James was ashore, he called on Victor to express his gratitude and that was the beginning of an unlikely, but mutual friendship. Victor was impressed at the mature use that twenty-year-old James was making of his authority as Second Master. He recognised something of himself at twenty in James' no-nonsense, albeit sometimes reckless, attitude to life.

Naturally, James had wanted to frequent Victor's establishment on this special occasion and he had given strict orders to his men that nobody was to be in any doubt that they were guests, not overlords, in Victor's place of business.

Victor was the perfect host. As a man who had only known daughters, he felt a sense of protectiveness towards James, who he knew had long been without a father-figure in his life. He had little time for most of the sailors who frequented his gin house, but James Neary was an unusual man: keenly aware of his duty to his Queen and country, he had learned to be open to and respectful of the different life led by the islanders. Partly out of a professional pride, but also out of genuine warmth for the young naval officer, Victor was determined to give James a birthday to remember. The rum never stopped flowing. The host organised a fun evening of cockfighting in the yard, and much hard-earned cash was lost in the proceedings. James was not a gambling man, but it cheered his heart to see his men so happy and content. James took charge when one of the new recruits, no more than thirteen years of age, engineered a fight between himself and the local undertaker. James was an able man to have in a fight, but on this occasion, like on many others, it was his tongue of authority and good humour that prevented any further trouble. The boy was dispatched to the market square to be flogged and the party continued.

 As the rum and other liquors took their hold, Victor, ever the businessman, summoned his daughter to the inn. Mistress Sophia, a handsome woman in her thirties, was the proprietress of the main street's whorehouse and she had brought a number of girls to Victor's to entertain the party guests, including, at James' request, Genevieve. James felt in his trousers pocket for the tin where his lambskin and oil-bottle resided. He'd given the younger boys the same counsel that he'd received, but it was up to them whether they chose to follow it. A man had to make his own decisions and take his own chances.

Well, James had taken his chances prudently and it had definitely been his lucky night. He grinned reminiscently, stretched and rose. He rinsed the sheath and then washed himself and dressed. There would be a next time and James' intention was that it would in the not too distant future. There had been other women in other ports, but none could hold a candle to Genevieve. James admired the fact that, like Victor and his daughter, Genevieve had a resourcefulness that had served her well during her harsh past on a sugar plantation and continued to allow her to flourish as she built a new life for herself. He knew that to her, he was not much more than just another customer, but he felt a liking for her as well as undeniable lust. He knew that there would never be more than casual liking between them, though.

He pondered briefly what it would be like to have a woman with whom you could share not just the pleasures of the bed and of a good breakfast, but your thoughts, your hopes and your worries. What it would be like to have a wife and – he felt a renewed warmth at the base of his belly – ride bareback. None of the women James had met on the island were what he would think of as wife material. A wife meant a home and Jamaica was not home.

Home was usually a long way from James's thoughts, but now he considered his three brothers, back in the grocer's shop. It had been five years since he had had any contact with them and James wondered which of the three brothers was currently winning the feud over who was to succeed their father in running the shop. Not in general a man of smugness, James leaned his elbows on the windowsill and thought that not one of his brothers could possibly imagine the life he was living now.

The navy was making a man out of him and he anticipated the many battles that awaited him in the long years still remaining of his service. He was mightily satisfied with the choices he had made. His life was devoted to serving Queen and country for at least the next ten years, and his overriding feeling was one of excitement. If his heart did not shrivel and coarsen with all the death and violence he was likely to encounter, one day he might open his heart fully to a wife. One day, but not yet. If his heart survived.

James recalled an evening, several months ago, spent with Victor. They had taken a small boat out for a fishing trip. It was a trip that they had made many times before. They often spent their evening in relaxed silence, both men content to let the fish and the smooth water heal the dark images that had taken root in their heads. The sea couldn't purge the ugliest of their memories, but it offered a temporary, calming respite. They had shared their experiences of the evil that men can do and knew that sometimes, the mind could only be cleansed by locking away the gruesome and giving oneself to the regulatory waves. After a night of rich pickings, James talked to Victor about matters of the soul and his fears of his heart becoming a wrinkled shell by the time that he was forty. Victor put his arms around James's shoulder and gently said:

"Our lives is a risk. To be a man of rich, filled heart or to be a man with a broken, withered shell has always been the choice. Ever since the good Lord walked this earth, man has wrestled with that dilemma. You're a good man, James Neary. You will make the right choice for you."

As the sun went down, the two close friends cooked their crayfish over the fire and reflected on matters of love and belief and courage.

A smell, not of crayfish but of johnnycakes, salt mackerel and mint tea, filled the air. This, thought James, was no time for reflection. It was a time for action - and time for breakfast. He straightened up from the windowsill and strode off to find out what his twenty-first year held for him.

13. Three Significant Days

There is a theory that you don't notice the most significant days of your life whilst they are actually happening. We only notice them, come the final day of reckoning, and even then, most of us aren't given the time for much self-reflection in that big moment. I think I've finally found a purpose for my green It book. It could come in very handy to make a record of my most significant days. Being the list anorak that I am, I would like to think that I could come up with my Top Ten list of most significant days. But to prevent this book from turning into an autobiography, I'm going to focus on three. The significance of them being significant will become clearer.

Part One

It is 10am on Monday 4th January 2019. I am in a gown and paper pants. I am in the hands of the anaesthetist. She's nice. Reassuring and knowledgeable in equal measures. What more could I ask? She encourages me to talk about myself, and I tell her that today my new book is being published. I had left home before my complimentary copies had arrived, so, I will have to wait a whole week before I will be able to hold a copy of my endeavours. The anaesthetist is interested and my vanity carries me through the next ten minutes as I describe the contents of the book and the process of putting the whole thing together. We even laugh. And the fact that she is fitting me up with an epidural, prior to having a small melon-sized tumour and a third of my bladder removed, becomes irrelevant.

A swing door opens and we are joined by another anaesthetist; this one will be attending to me during the surgery. As the door opens, I catch a fleeting glimpse of the operating theatre on the other side. A quartet of indistinguishable figures in blue gowns and masks and hairnets are looking busy in the advent of my arrival. The door closes. I forget about the book. I am quite alone.

Five hours later, I wake up in the intensive care ward. I have been pre-warned that I would wake up in the intensive care ward, so it isn't a shock. But it is shocking. I am in a bed at the far end of the ward. I am at right angles to all the other beds, so I've got a good view of several other patients in varying states of pre-death. I don't feel in a state of impending death. I feel alert and even, perky. I can't feel any pain. A nurse speaks to me, and welcomes me onto the ward and I find that I can string a coherent sentence together. I start to take in my body and notice how wired up I am. I can't quite see it in its full glory, but I am aware of the catheter bag, dangling over the side of the bed. I nervously pull back the sheet and see where the other end of the catheter is going. Another big bag at the side of the bed reveals that I am being flushed out. That bag is directly plugged into my bladder. There is a morphine drip that I don't appear to be attached to. I wonder how problematic it may be to readjust my position and whilst I ponder the predicament, a nurse appears and says: "Let's move you up a bit." Elevated, I have got a better view of the ward. Compared to my fellow intensive peers, I am in the Upper Circle whilst they are flat out in the stalls. I am not quite so alone.

There is an almost silent hustle and bustle about the ward. Everyone is attending to something life or death, but there are no discernable noises. People talk quietly, like they are in church. Even the beeps from the myriad machines seem muted. It might feel like an honourable preparation for an anticipated death, but it curiously feels very alive at the same time. Staff smile. Staff have time. I haven't seen the doctor yet, but I know that I am not dying.

Six months earlier, I was alone in a Torquay hotel bedroom and feeling that I might be dying. It was the night of England's World Cup semi-final game against Croatia, but I spent most of the match in agony, on the toilet. I tried to reassure myself that I had eaten something that had disagreed with me ("No you haven't") and I kept checking myself in the mirror. I was a bodybuilder, and after a year of absolutely nailing my training and my diet, I was looking extremely hench. The idea that something might be terribly wrong with me internally didn't square with the buff figure looking back at me. So, I didn't square it and the next day, despite feeling like my guts were rotting away, I was back in the hotel gym. No pain, no gain eh?

Over the next few weeks, I affected an unconscious blindness. I mistook my jaundice for the remnants of my Torquay tan. I explained my dramatic weight loss with the certainty that my diet and supplementation programme was doing its job. I even reassured myself that despite my stools having turned a pale grey, my body was still adjusting itself to my new, healthy, food intake. Excusing away the pain was less easy though. I shut myself away. I could manage this all alone.

It took two months for the CT appointment to come through. And three days before the scan, the unbearable pain in my gut, stopped. Suddenly, like it had never been. My normal colour returned. My shit started to look like shit again. I was tempted to cancel the CT appointment.

"You have a large, sizeable, cancerous tumour in your urachus. The good news is we believe that the cancer is contained within your urachus, so removal will be straightforward. It has been growing for many years and unfortunately, the weight and pressure of the tumour has damaged a significant section of your bladder. But don't worry, we'll be able to remove the damaged area."

You don't forget statements like that. Like you never forget the lyrics of Squeeze's 'Up The Junction.' I can remember the diagnosis word for word. The words were delivered after the CT scan, after an exploratory operation, and after the very unexpected heart attack, four days after the exploratory operation. I recovered speedily from those annoying interruptions to my usual life, and although the word "cancer" had been hanging in the air for three months, it wasn't my main pre-occupation after hearing the (potentially) life changing diagnosis. My first thought was: "Shit. That puts the mockers on the competition next Spring." I was due to turn sixty in March 2019, and my planning and focus for the previous years, was that I would be eligible to compete in the "Seniors" class at my first bodybuilding competition. Ten years earlier, I had planned to make my competitive debut in the Over 50s class, but once again, pesky life got in the way, and my posing trunks gathered dust in my chest of drawers for a whole decade. I was furious that the cancer was preventing that dream from happening for a second time. My therapist termed that my "displacement activity", but she had never witnessed my magnificent double lat spread pose, so what did she know?

I wasn't interested in the cancer. I'm still not. I don't have any interest in telling a cancer story. I don't like all the "hero" and "battle" language associated with cancer stories. My great friend, Shelley wrote an incredible blog during her cancer experience and titled it, "Tangling With Cancer". That is the way to do it. The only time that I became disturbed by the diagnosis was over the Christmas holiday, two weeks before my tangle with the anaesthetist. It was the only time that I cried over those few months. I cried on Christmas Day when the thought hit me that it might be my very last Christmas with Steven. Every tub of Cheeselets and every new Paul

Heaton CD, felt like a punch in my stomach. But I wasn't alone.

After three days in intensive care, I was "stepped down" to a regular ward, and then the full degradation of my predicament came home to roost. Despite witnessing several deaths whilst I was on the intensive care ward, the humanity and professionalism of the staff had cocooned me from certain realities about my current condition. I had only moved six floors up the hospital complex, but it was another universe, in terms of safety and kindness. I learned what it was like to be truly vulnerable. I understand what it was like to be seen as just a case. And I wouldn't wish that on my worst enemy. In a crowded, bustling ward, I had never felt so alone.

The three days on Tudor Ward had humiliations in hourly doses. Being scolded because my urine bag had overfilled. Being scolded because I had emptied my urine bag without informing a nurse. Shitting on the floor because I wasn't fit enough to run the length of the ward, to the toilet in time. Being encouraged to get dressed, but being unable to bend down deeply enough to put my socks on, as the thirty nine staples in my gut were restricting my ability to achieve a solitary sit-up. Gagging uncontrollably at the sight and the smell of a sausage hot-pot. It was a succession of indignities that my twenty first century male pride found impossible to handle.

When I come to write my final story, I am sure that the fifteen minutes in the anaesthetist's chamber will feature in the ten most significant moments of my life. I think I know why. My Dad died in January and my Mum died in February, so that time of the year carries an extra emotional punch. I moved away from Southall in 1983, but remained registered with the same doctors and dentists, well into the nineties. Such is the power of the subconscious that for many years, during January or February, I would feel ill or have teeth problems. This would, of course, give me cause to return to Southall to visit one of the practices. It took me a long time to understand that I was doing this, in a perverse way to try and stay close to my parents. I no longer contrive a winter visit to Southall but there is a part of me that still cannot quite let go. That showed up around the operation. I am sure that my lack of fear about the cancer and the heart attack comes from that drive to still be with them. To put it bluntly, that reunion with my parents could only be achieved through my death. And sod those that are living, who care about me. Thankfully, there is another part of me that took precedent in January 2019.

I see myself as quite practical and being alive feels better than being dead. And, going back to the It book days, I am quite an expert in being alone. This goes way beyond introversion. I have a tenuous grasp of phenomenological philosophy and know that 'aloneness' is one of the four givens of existence. Prior to January 2019, I had read about it, debated it, even lectured on the subject, but a heart attack and a melon-sized tumour brings it perilously close. I have always noticed that 'life goes on' aspect of funerals. I've buried my parents, my wife and my baby and I am always struck that during the journey to the crematorium, the world is populated by people going about their daily business. When the hospital visitors go home and the nightshift staff clock on, you come face to face with aloneness in its most raw.

During one of the long evenings in hospital, I thought about my great-grandfather, William Culley. Did he have time to muster any final thoughts that afternoon, as he released Job and Esther into the sky, one final time? Did he look to the sky as they took flight? What did the sky look like as the gunfire started?

William Culley was wounded at Diamond Hill, but six months later, he was back in action, in a new unit. I am now cancer free but my abdominal wall didn't repair successfully after the surgery and I've been left with a huge, unsightly hernia. It requires another operation. There is a long waiting list.

I do like to entertain the notion though, that my eventual introduction to the world of bodybuilding competition (Senior Class) could still happen when I am sixty five.

I am thinking of Linda, and her closing scene in Blood Brothers:

"Her dreams were not forgotten.
Just wrapped and packed away.

In the hope that she could take them down.

And dust them off, one day".

Part Two

9th June 2011. The Royal Courts of Justice. The last stop of a long, eighteen month journey and the day that would start another change in my life direction.

On 30th December 2009, I arranged for Steven to spend three nights at this respite centre, as I was struggling with a nasty bout of flu. It didn't feel like a big deal at the time. Steven had been going to the centre for over a year and was fairly tolerant of the place. It was an arrangement that social services had repeatedly encouraged me to do. The following day, the social worker moved Steven to an assessment and treatment unit and kept him there for the next 359 days. The council's plan, as the year progressed, was to never let him come back home, but to move him even further away, to a long stay hospital in Wales. Their reasoning was that his behaviour was too challenging to be cared for at home. This is what happens regularly to people with learning disabilities. There is a huge industry invested in making money and taking control over the lives of learning disabled people. Steven was (and, is) just one of many thousands of people for whom the State and the private care system only see the person as a commodity.

We hit an intransigent obstacle from the second day of Steven being away. He didn't react very well to the move. This should have come as no surprise to anyone. His distress and confusion manifested in the type of behaviour that shocked anyone who knew him on a day to day basis. The poor guy was frightened. The council used his distressed behaviour as their reason why he must not be allowed to return home. My argument was that his behaviour was a sign of his distress; let him come home and the behaviour will cease. That stalemate lasted for the best part of a year. That's how we treat human beings in the 21st century.

The council spent the whole of 2010, compiling their case. There was no assessment. There was no treatment apart from introducing Steven to a life-threatening medication regime that he didn't need. They framed all their reports and logs to present Steven as a dangerous individual, whilst refusing to acknowledge their role in turning him into the person they were seeing through their risk averse and very blinkered spectacles. They refused to see Steven as a human being. He has a wonderful talent that he draws upon when he realises that he is not being able to make himself understood, verbally. He has an encyclopaedic knowledge of music and he will find a song that he hopes will best communicate his message. Everyday, when the manager of the unit arrived for work, Steven would shake his hand and sing to him, the Queen song, 'I Want To Break Free.' The staff resolutely refused to acknowledge the message in the song and dismissed it as a sign of "autistic echolalia."

One major stumbling block, throughout the year, was my pride in Steven's stoicism and invention. That seriously pissed the professionals off. On the night that one of Steven's favourite bands, Take That, reunited with Robbie Williams on the X Factor to perform their classic, 'The Flood', Steven saw a small window of opportunity, and escaped. He was in his pyjamas and ran barefoot, for over a mile. He got to within spitting distance of his mother's home when he was found. The following day, he told me what his plan had been:

"Steven Neary was going to Julie Neary's house. Julie Neary will speak to Mark Neary on the phone. Mark Neary will come in the car and take Steven Neary back home."

It was a great plan and nearly succeeded. And I was in awe at his invention and courage. The professionals were on the back foot and furious, because their whole plan was built on their assertion that Steven lacks mental capacity. He played a blinder in driving a huge hole through their pet theory.

We nervously launched the "Get Steven Home" campaign. It led to a lot of press and media attention and our case, quickly developed a public profile. Social media was, by and large, on Steven's side and there is no doubt that the scrutiny applied by the BBC, The Independent, The Times and many others, put a renewed pressure on the council. Inevitably, they pushed back, painting a very unfair, and untrue picture of Steven, but it was inkeeping with their preoccupation of seeing him as an object.

Our first appearance in the High Court was in December 2010 and the hearing lasted, just three hours. I was in the witness box for less than thirty minutes and one question from the judge made me sob:

"Mr Neary. If I let Steven come home today, tell me what his life would be like."

I cried because it was the first time in a whole year that anyone had been interested enough in Steven, to see him as a man with a life worth living. It took the judge no time at all to make his ruling: Steven could return home immediately.

Six months later, we were back in the same courtroom, this time under Justice Peter Jackson. Steven's barrister had pushed for the legality of the year long detention to be examined and this necessitated a week long hearing in May 2010. Steven was legally represented, but I wasn't, so I had to present my own case and cross examine all the witnesses. It was nerve wracking, but I had to keep reminding myself that the pressure was off me and Steven. The spotlight was off us, but firmly on the council and I had an important role to play in exposing their duplicity. There is something inherently theatrical about the High Court and it would have been easy to put on my Henry Fonda costume, but I think I did okay.

On a blistering hot day in June, we reconvened for Justice Jackson's ruling. The council had used a little known piece of legislation called the Deprivation of Liberty Safeguards

(DoLS) to keep Steven in the unit, and the judge ruled that all four DoLS that the council had served on Steven throughout 2010 had been unlawful. He also judged that the council had breached Steven's article five and article eight rights, under the Human Rights Act. The council couldn't have got things more wrong. It was a bittersweet victory.

In his judgment, Justice Jackson turned his attention onto me. He described me as "an unusual man" who "can be proud of the way in which he stood up for his son's interests." He also said that, "with a lesser parent, Steven would have faced a life in public care that he did not want, and does not need." He was right. I am proud of that. But much more so, I am proud of Steven. I am proud of the way that he was able to withstand the distress of a year of being kept away from everything he knows. All his anchors were snatched away, but he survived. And in the years that have followed, I am proud that he has had the courage and the imagination to build a new life for himself. A life that gives him meaning and keeps him safe. I marvel at his fortitude and get a lot of strength from his strength.

At one point during his judgment, Justice Jackson referred to Magna Carta. As he explained the relevance of this piece of law from 1297, he cut through all the defenses that I had constructed over the difficult, preceding eighteen months. When history, your history as part of humankind is presented to you at such close hand, the impact is very powerful. Well, it was to me. I felt viscerally, the timeline, my timeline, going back eight hundred years. I had been feeling quite alone that day, but now I wasn't. Steven Neary and Mark Neary were living descendants of Magna Carta.

I had no idea, as I stood on the steps of the High Court being interviewed by the press and the television crews, how much my life would change that day. I knew that the judgment had been launched into the universe and I would never know how many people's lives might be changed by it. Quite quickly, I became "a voice." I have spent the past ten years, speaking at all manner of public events. Initially, I was booked to tell the Get Steven Home story, but more recently, the subject matter has shifted and it seems like the small world of social care believes that I have something worth saying.

And I belatedly became a writer. Friends encouraged me to write a book about the year. It was well received and I've since gone on to write another four books. My blog has a loyal band of followers.

In 1976, I was doing my A-Levels and my plan was to go to university, which would hopefully lead to a career in journalism. In the February of that year, my mother died and I believed that my place was at home with my family. I don't regret that decision. It only took another thirty five years to become a writer.

Part Three.

1976.

This is how cocooned I was. It had never occurred to me,
until a week before she died, that my Mum had probably had
cancer for about nine years. There is a famous family photo of
us at Pontins holiday camp in 1967. My sister is in her
pushchair. Dad and Mum are standing next to each other and
I am kneeling down, next to Jayne. When I look at the
photograph now, the first thing that I see is the small dressing
on Mum's shin. She had a wound in her leg for a long time
and she would regularly have the hole scraped out by Doctor
Pragnell. Nobody ever mentioned the word "cancer", but after
she died, my Dad told me that he believed that the strange
mass on her leg was the beginning of her cancer journey.

In 1971, she had an operation to remove a kidney. Once
again, cancer wasn't talked about. I remember walking
unannounced into her bedroom one day when she was half-
dressed. She had several odd, black arrows drawn on her
back. I knew that she was having radiotherapy, but had no
idea why, or what that entailed. In hindsight, I can see that
the arrows were the directions for the radiologist, temporarily
tattooed on her back.

My first realisation that something was seriously wrong was
at the tail end of the school summer holiday in 1975. We went
for a family day out to the open air pool at Windsor. Mum

didn't go in the water, but stayed in the spectators' grandstand. When I came out of the changing room, I found Dad and Jayne bending over her. She had collapsed. We had to carry her back to the station, to catch our train. The deterioration was pretty quick from that day. Within two months, she had lost the use of her legs completely and had to use a wheelchair. For months, Mum had been looking forward to Christmas, because Uncle Albert had organised a four night break for us and all the extended family, in Bournemouth. Two days before we were due to travel, Mum announced that she and Dad would be staying at home, but encouraged me and Jayne to go with the rest of the family. It seems so clear now that Mum and Dad were still desperately in love and wanted to spend one last Christmas together. On that first night in Bournemouth, as we sat eating dinner, the waiter approached Uncle Albert and informed him that he had an urgent phone call. For the few minutes that he was away, one by one, the older relatives started crying, as they feared the worst. Upon his return, Uncle Albert announced solemnly that their eldest brother, Uncle Charlie, had suffered a major heart attack in his lorry and had died. It was a double shock. Everyone expected the news to be about Mum, but any relief was lost in the awful, unexpected news about their brother, and our uncle.

In the third week of January 1976, 'Mamma Mia' entered the UK Top 10 and Mum entered hospital. The week before she died, my Dad tried to prepare me for her passing, but in his distressed bravery, he didn't exactly say that she was going to die; just that she wouldn't be coming home again. For a brief few hours, I wrestled with the confused illusion of having, in several years' time, to visit Mum in hospital on my wedding day, so that she could see me in my best suit. By the time I woke up the next morning, that fantasy had been replaced with the sadder reality.

I still couldn't picture how we would live without her. Mum was such a significant figure in the entire family. She was the youngest of six siblings and may have been an accidental baby. There was quite a large age difference between her and her next eldest sister. In fact, she was nearer in age to her nephews and nieces than she was to most of her brothers and sisters, so she became the bridge between two generations of Worleys. Her wedding album illustrates this; of her three bridesmaids, one was her sister and the other two were her nieces. The nieces never called her "Auntie" either, but they wouldn't have dreamed of not using that title when speaking of the other sisters: Wilky, Rose and Hilda. Her sisters didn't mother her, though. She always seemed very much an equal.

Mum had a similar effect on Dad's family too. Perhaps all families need one person, willing to take on the role of providing the family glue? It was certainly true that after her death, the number of family get-togethers decreased significantly. On Sundays, we had had an unofficial rota for visiting various arms of the family. Although she would never have admitted this, I'm sure that her favourite people to visit were my Dad's sister, Auntie Eve; and Eve's husband,

Uncle Tom. In particular, she revelled in Uncle Tom's company. I don't think the attraction was physical, at all. Uncle Tom was a doppelganger for Charlie Hawtrey, from the Carry On films. I think the attraction was that they could make each other laugh hysterically. I liked those visits too. It took him about three years, but Uncle Tom built a model village in their back garden. It had everything: a stream, a parade of shops, a castle, even a cricket pavilion. It was a brilliant piece of design engineering.

I don't want to paint a picture of Mum as a sickly, angel figure, because she wasn't. As she died when I was sixteen, I only ever saw her through a child's eyes and one of my deepest yearnings is for the adult relationship that I never got to have with her. My picture of her is naturally limited in scope and sentiment.

Mum died on a Saturday morning. This was at the time that I was working on the cooked meats counter at Fine Fare. I left for work that day with no inkling of what was to follow. The penny didn't even drop when I came home for lunch. Auntie Wilky and Auntie Phil had arrived to cook me egg and chips, as Dad had dashed off to the hospital. When I got back to the flat that evening, Dad was home and Uncle Bob was by his side, to offer moral support. Jayne was staying with Mum's best friend for the weekend. I can remember little from that night, or from the next few days, apart from some jigsaw pieces of sadness and bewilderment. That same Saturday evening, Dad and I went out for some fish and chips and nearly got mowed down by the heavy Western Road traffic. I remember school on the Monday morning. Mr Curtis, my English teacher, chatted to me gently in his office, whilst Mr Faure, the head of the sixth form, broke the news to my classmates. A sweet memory is of Jim Humble, the groundsman at Southall Football Club. He turned up and presented me with one of those old-fashioned wooden rattles, which had been in his family for generations. I had admired it for years and he had given it a fresh lick of red and white paint, before handing it on to me. And that's about it for memories. I guess we just kept on keeping on.

The significant day was the funeral, the Friday after Mum's death. I didn't own a suit, so I wore Dad's rather gaudy, Tony Curtis style checked jacket and a pair of brown, Crimplene slacks. I may have felt like a five year old on the inside, but on the outside, I looked like Ted Rodgers. Over the next couple of years, I was to become first a soul boy, then a punk, before finding my true spiritual identity - a mod. But on the day we said our farewells to Beryl Neary, I resembled a spunky Bobby Crush.

The mourners were assembling in speedily increasing numbers and our small flat was starting to feel claustrophobic. Never at ease with small talk, I decided that I needed some fresh air. Our front garden was covered in flowers. I was in year one of my French A-Level and had a vocabulary book that had been written circa 1940. I loved it. The language was hilariously outdated. I used to drive Mr

Hart, the French teacher, crazy by including some of the most archaic, wooden phrases into every essay. One of my favourites was, "That bed of flowers was an orgy of colour, last week." It was the "last week" tagged on the end that creased me up, every time. For once, I could use the phrase appropriately, because our garden was an orgy of colour that day.

Whilst I was looking aimlessly at the wreaths, my cousin Carol turned up. She is ten years older than I am, so when I was growing up in the 1960s, she was off, being a teenager and doing terribly exciting teenage things. Over the previous few years, Carol and Mum had become very close, so I had started to know her better. Carol walked into our garden and, without saying anything, enveloped me in a massive bear-hug. It was the first hug I'd had since Dad had broken the news, six days earlier. I can still feel that hug. A few weeks earlier, Carol had been at the hotel in Bournemouth and it was with her, on Christmas Day, that Jayne and I had sat, to open our presents. That was a metaphorical hug; this was a real hug. It was a Worley hug.

I've only got one other memory of funeral day and it was pure Joe Orton comedy that Beryl Neary née Worley would have loved. We got back from the funeral and had a small wake at Auntie Rose's. Then Uncle Albert announced that he had booked a table at The Swan and Bottle, which was a kind of Berni Inn before Berni Inns became fashionable. We split into three carloads: Uncle Albert driving one; Carol driving the second; and Kath bringing up the rear. I was in Uncle Albert's car with Dad, Jayne and Auntie Rose. Halfway there, Uncle Albert decided that the car needed filling up. As we were exiting the petrol station, he spotted a car wash, and said:

"Ooh. Let's wash the gloom of the day off. Just two minutes."

He drove the car into the wash. The rollers came down. The foam started spraying and water appeared from every direction. The next thing we knew, there was an almighty clunk and the rollers dropped even further, before stopping with a thud on the car bonnet.

"Fuck," said Uncle Albert, "We're trapped."

Like a mourning Greek Chorus, one by one, we started to shout, "HELP." There were plenty of people, milling about on the forecourt, but nobody appeared to hear us. The rollers had stopped rolling, the foam had stopped foaming, but the water was still pounding the windows and the roof. And then, as casually and as authoritatively as you like, Uncle Albert wound down the window, shouted "Help, you sods," and wound the window straight back up again. Within seconds, we were rescued.

Ten minutes later, we arrived at The Swan and Bottle. The other two cars had gone on ahead and Carol and the rest of the Worleys were already at our table, ordering the first round of drinks. As we walked in, everyone stood up and said in unison,

"Whatever has happened to you lot?"

In the few seconds that Uncle Albert had wound down the car window to summon assistance, we had all got soaked to the skin. Seated in the passenger seat, Auntie Rose had caught the worst of it and it was months before her perm recovered. I learned the painful life lesson that crimplene is the worst material for soaking up rainwater. We all stood as Carol proposed a toast to Beryl and as we sat back down, five of us started off a symphony of squelching. Somebody said,

"Beryl would have loved to have seen you in that car wash. You'd have never heard the last of it."

Between you and me, I think it was Beryl, up there in Heaven, who caused the rollers to get stuck. For a joke. I wouldn't put it past her.

14: The Pigeon Man

Exhibit label, attached to Exhibit 212, from the Military Intelligence Museum, Shefford.

Letter found amongst the kit of Private William Culley, Cape Cycling Corps, after he was killed in action on 18th April 1901.

Private Culley (1867 to 1901) was born in Ditchingham, Norfolk and married Mary White in 1866. They had two children: William Junior and Annie.

Private Culley was a career soldier. He saw two spells of action in the second Boer War. He was wounded in June 1900 at Diamond Hill whilst serving with the 10th Hussars. On recovering, he was transferred to the Cape Colony Cycling Corps in January 1901.

As can be gathered from Pte. Culley's letter, the Cycling Corps was a vital part of the British Army's developing Military Intelligence network. Due to the sensitive military nature of some of the content, the letter was retained in Intelligence archives and Private Culley's wife never received or read it.

ARE **YOU** FOND OF CYCLING?
IF SO
WHY NOT CYCLE
FOR THE KING?

RECRUITS WANTED
By the S. Midland Divisional Cyclist Company
(Must be 19, and willing to serve abroad)
CYCLES PROVIDED. Uniform and Clothing issued
on enlistment.

Application in person or by letter to
Cyclists, The Barracks, Gloucester.

BAD TEETH NO BAR.

19th March 1901

My Dearest Mary,

How are you, my sweet Wife? I am so sorry that it has been over a month since my last letter, but it has been a particularly trying time here at Orange River (more of that anon).

What marvellous news you spoke of in your last letter about my darling little Annie. Although, I suspect she is not so little anymore. Curse this war for preventing me from seeing both my children grow up. My heart took kindly to the notion of my little girl learning to play the piano. Where does she get that rare talent from? I certainly cannot recall any person in my family having such a gift. In the dank, black nights here, I like to imagine Annie playing a soft melody to me when I eventually return home.

I was less overjoyed at the mention of Annie and young Billy spending time with the stable boys in the mews. These boys can be very rough, both in their actions and in their language, and I would hope that Billy is taking his responsibilities as the elder Brother with all the seriousness that we have tried to instill in him. I suppose it is the fecklessness of their age that sees them both drawn to the rougher parts of Kensington. Do you remember your Mother, boasting quite shamelessly to her neighbours when we first got our London home? I can hear her saying, "My Mary is going up in the world and no Cockney ragamuffin will ever sully her life". I am chuckling as I write these words. Your family embraced our London move whilst my family feared that it would lead to us getting ideas above our station. How little do they understand you, my precious one?

What a stroke of good fortune it was for your Cousin to get that small flat in Thorpe Mews. It will mean good company for you. I hardly need to state the obvious, but I saw so little of our new London home before my posting, but I do believe that I remember Thorpe Mews. I have a remembrance of walking the children to the park one Sunday afternoon whilst you were ailing, and I was amused at little Annie's questioning stares at the maidservants and the grooms, taking their Sunday constitutionals. And there, my dearest, is the essence of our new life. If we are to have the smart grooms; then we must also have the stable boys.

Oh Mary. I yearn to stroll with you along by the nice houses. Our hands held tightly together. Those thoughts can raise my spirits during this bleak, bloody war in Africa, where one day unfolds as tortuous as all the previous ones, as will surely do, the next.

I try, my darling, to keep my correspondence to you, light and positive. I do not want to fret you as I know how hard it is to be on your own with only your imagination raising terrible pictures of your husband's war, many thousands of miles away.

Sometimes, my mood is very low, but I am cheered on a daily basis by the pigeons. Have you given any more thought to my suggestion of breeding pigeons when I return to London? It would be no trouble at all to build a small loft in the back yard. And I would tend to their every need, with no call upon your time for assistance.

You asked why the carrier pigeons have become the responsibility of the cycling corps, as it appears so unlikely. I jest not, Mary, but the answer is simple. The horses are intolerant of the pigeons and do not take kindly to their noise or movement whilst being carried on the saddle. So, transporting them between stations can be dangerous to the birds and can only be performed on bicycle. I am sure that Billy and Annie will be greatly amused by that piece of war news. It takes time for the pigeons to be ready to serve King and country, so it has become the job of Archie Anderson and I to train and tend to the birds before they commence active service.

Here is my little secret, Mary. I have taken a particular shine to two of the pigeons, who I have christened Job, after your admirable Father, and Esther, after my poor, late Sister. They make quite a pair, I can tell you. They have opened my eyes to the skies again. Much of the time at wartime, you are either looking straight down or straight ahead. Both in full concentration for any danger. One has no need to look up, so you don't. But watching these two doughty birds as they take flight, my heart takes flight too and before I know it, my mind is back on the farm in Ditchingham and I can temporarily imagine that this blasted war is over. Excuse my coarse language, Mary. I must sound like one of the stable boys in Thorpe Mews. Archie jokes that I am better suited to the asylum than the bunker, because I like to talk to Job and Esther. I've told them about you, my precious dear, and I like to pretend that one day, I will set them free, and they will take the long journey to Kensington, carrying my love back to you. Do I sound the fool, Mary? When Archie is engaged with his ablutions and out of earshot, I like to tell the pigeons about my dreams for the future. I do not want anyone to hear what those dreams are, even you, dear Mary, because my greatest fear is that I will not live to see them being realised. I trust the birds though, and it is some comfort that there is someone that I can release the burden to.

Besides tending to the pigeons, our other main duty is to service and repair the bicycles. My goodness, Mary, you would not believe the toll this African terrain takes on the old bicycles. I had to cycle with a message to the Corporal's base last week. It could have been no more than forty miles. I half expected never to arrive as the wretched bicycle kept buckling and falling into disrepair. For the final, couple of miles, I ended up carrying the thing, instead of it carrying me. With the bike, my kit and my weapons, I was weighed down a ton. My back was playing me up so much; I must have looked like I walk as an ostrich does. To make our tasks even harder, the tools we have been equipped with to carry out the repairs are of very poor quality. If I was a betting man, I would be loath to gamble the odds on what might fail the troops first: the bicycle frame or the spanners needed to repair the frames.

Whilst cycling to Calvinia last week, I was bolstered heartily by a fond memory. It was a memory I hadn't recalled for many years. I presume that it was the bicycle, the vast open spaces and the roasting sun, but I was taken back to the time when I was stationed in Dorchester. Those many times that I would cycle with as much vigour as I could muster, along the coastal roads, to spend a precious Sunday afternoon with you in Kilmington. The ride never took any physical toll, because I always had the joy of your beautiful face with its crown of shining, black hair to look forward to. The anticipation of seeing you, dearest Mary, was all the energy a man needed to undertake such a rambling journey. I must remember to use that same energy to boost me the next time I am given a mission to bicycle the pigeons across the fields to base.

I have some sad news to report. You may recall in one of my earlier letters to you, I told you about the wonderful cakes that young Albert Jackson used to receive from home. Like a lot of Albert's, he was referred to as Nobby, and what a card he was. He had high hopes of making his living as a footballer when this war is over, and in my humble, and probably ignorant opinion, I am sure that he would have succeeded. When we had an occasional kick about, there was not a single soldier in the corps who could get the ball off him. You would have sworn that he had magnets in his boots. To be frank, it became quite tiresome after a while, but it wasn't just me who could see that Nobby had potential. He had some stories of his life back in Newcastle that would have us clutching our sides with laughter. Archie never found them funny and would call them "tall stories", but Nobby had a way about him, that you never really bothered whether the tales were true or not. The reward was in the laughter.

Anyway, the sad news is that Nobby died last Thursday. He set out with a couple of the other lads to provide cover for the medical corps. There had been several injuries during the last push and Nobby was amongst those sent to their aid. I was excused for the day as I had work to do with Esther. From the stories that I've heard, Nobby became separated from the rest of the boys. They found him three hours later. He was barely conscious and one of his legs was missing. But do you know, Mary? The cheeky bounder survived for another four days. The pain must have been excruciating. It was the fever that got him in the end. One sees life very differently out here, Mary. Not so long ago, I would have been saddened beyond words by such a happening to one of my friends. I still feel sad for Nobby, and his poor mother but I feel cheered too. It was for the best that the tropics did for him in the final count. He wouldn't have liked not being able to play football anymore. A man must be able to have his dreams. Taking those dreams away is cruelty itself.

We have got a few more days here and then we are being moved to Pretoria to provide reinforcements to protect the railway line. I know that you find this hard to hear, my wonderful wife, but I am pleased that we will finally be seeing some proper action, after such a long spell of never-ending boredom. To fight was the reason that I signed up all those years ago and every one of us men relishes the day when we put everything on the line for victory. I pray to God that Job and Esther are ready for their part in the action before we have to leave. I could not bear to have to wring their necks if the officers deem them to be unready.

I will sign off now, my sweet. Give Annie a big soldier hug from me. And try your hardest to persuade Billy to reconsider his ambition to follow in his father's footsteps. After this war, the world will open up for young men like Billy and he won't need the army to give him his sense of purpose. I want both my children to live long, happy lives, without the sword of war hanging over them.

Do not worry Mary. I will be home in your arms before you know it. My army days will soon be over and we can look forward to our golden future, with or without a pigeon loft. I trust you'll appreciate my little joke to end on. It is a poor substitute for the kiss that I so want to give you.

Yours, today and forever.

Private William Culley (23899)

15. The Institution

I know very little about my Uncle Frank. Even though he only died two years before I was born, he was never talked about within the family. Well, not in front of me, anyway. The first time I learned of his existence was in 1997, forty years after he died. These days, Frank would be described as having a "learning disability." The one record that I have managed to trace about Uncle Frank that refers to his disability, has him labelled as "a retard."

One of the nagging questions for me about Uncle Frank is, why was he airbrushed from the family history? A number of people have suggested "shame" as an explanation and I accept that for people of that generation, and that class, shame about all manner of things, often hanged heavy. But shame doesn't quite fit the bill, for me. I was told a lovely story about my parents which indicates that shame would not have been a driving factor for them. Around the time of Uncle Frank moving away from the family home in Southall, another dilemma faced the Neary family, around disability. My Dad's sister, Auntie Phil, had two sons, who in 1950s parlance were termed as being "deaf and dumb." The common consensus at the time was that boys like that, couldn't live at home and in fact, would flourish in an institutional setting. There would have been a lot of pressure from the doctors and the social workers on the family to pursue that sort of arrangement. I don't envy my Auntie Phil and Uncle Geoff having to make that decision, and they were both the type of people who would have accepted the professionals' opinions as gospel. There is certainly a sense that the elder Nearys agreed with the clinicians. If there was any dissent, or at least, another perspective, that would have come from my parents. Both my mum and my dad were the youngest in their families, by a long way. They may have been afterthought, or accidental babies. Perhaps because they were from a slightly different generation, they took a different stance and put forward a case for Phillip and Gordon to say and to be educated and live in Southall. Mum and Dad even enrolled at night school to learn sign language in an attempt to show the family that communication was possible. Despite my parents' efforts, both boys were sent to a residential school for the deaf in Margate and stayed there until they were sixteen, when they eventually returned home. Part of the ethos of the school was that the pupils would learn a trade and Gordon went on to have a successful career as a car mechanic and rally cross driver. Again, revealing an open attitude towards disability, my Dad fixed Phillip up with a job in the factory where he worked at the time. As a small boy, I would sit and watch in fascination as dad and Phillip carried out whole conversations in signing. As no words were spoken, I hadn't a clue what they were discussing, but as they were both Arsenal supporters, I suspect that Charlie George was on the agenda. This doesn't sound like the actions of someone who might be ashamed of having a learning disabled brother.

Perhaps, there was a difference in attitudes between learning disabilities and physical disabilities. But Phillip cut across both those areas, so I can't see it carrying too much weight in my family.

I have one photo of Uncle Frank and it is revealing from a psychological perspective. Not his psychology: more perhaps about the family's psychology, or even the camera man's. The photo is of the large group assembling at my parent's wedding. It's obvious that the positioning of all the guests had been carefully thought out. Nearys to the left and the Worleys to the right. The front row is all the children, again positioned according to their birth tribes. The ages range from six to sixteen. Smack, bang in the middle of all the Neary children is Uncle Frank. Although he is crouched on one knee, he towers over all the other children. He must have been in his early thirties at the time. There is no way that he could have been taken physically for a child. Sixty years on, it looks offensively incongruous.

My theory about why Uncle Frank was never talked about has less to do with shame, and more to do with death. Death was more of a taboo in my family, and causing upset to the elders by talking about death, was certainly frowned upon. Not just Uncle Frank. I was astounded a couple of years ago when I discovered the story about the Farwells. My Auntie Hilda's husband was Albert Farwell and in 1942, six members of his family, including both his parents, were killed when a bomb fell on their house in Portland. The family had gathered for the wedding of one of the Farwell sons and the new bride was also one of the bomb's victims. Dorset legend has it that Agatha Christie, living in nearby Devon, heard about the incident and used it as the kicking off point for her 1945 novel, "Taken At The Flood." There is even a large memorial to the Farwell family in Portland's main square. I came along seventeen years later, and grew up with many of the survivors of this tragedy, but it was never mentioned. Likewise, nobody ever talked about the death of Dad's brother, Uncle Reg, apart from the occasional, reverential look at his war medals.

One last piece of evidence to support my death vs. disability theory is that my Nan, Emma Fleetwood/Worley had a couple of spells in St Bernards Lunatic Asylum which didn't appear to disarrange the family at all. It was talked about quite openly. What did disarrange the family though was that she died in St Bernards Lunatic Asylum. It was drilled into me from a very young age that mentioning Nan's death was a complete no-no because it would be too upsetting for some of the family members. There must have been a peculiar hierarchy of taboos at the time. Being in a lunatic asylum was not to be boasted about, but it was okay to be talked about in a hushed whisper. Dying in a lunatic asylum was a total no go area and had to be preserved as a terrible family secret. I like the Alan Bennett line that all families have secrets and the secret is that their secrets are no different from any other families' secrets.

The other question about Uncle Frank that I have sought an answer to is, why was he moved to Derby for the final two years of his life? Was the timing important? And did the move precipitate his early demise in any way? I suspect the answers are probably pragmatic. Both my Nan and Granddad were in their mid seventies at the time of Frank's move in 1955. I imagine that caring for Uncle Frank would have required a lot of energy. Judging by the wedding photo, he was quite a big man. My Dad was the last of my grandparent's children to leave home, when he got married in 1953 and the other son, Uncle Stan had emigrated to Australia in 1954. All of the four Neary daughters had married and were bringing up families of their own. Perhaps the responsibility had become too much in my grandparent's old age.

Or perhaps, social services were no different back then than they are these days, with their absolute certainty that learning disabled people must be living independently from their families in order to prepare them for their parent's eventual demise. Ever since Steven was sixteen, I have had social workers badgering me that Steven should move on so that he will cope better with my death when it happens. I think it is a form of unconscious discrimination. Nobody would dream of suggesting such a thing to a non disabled person. And it is as pointless, as it is cruel. Nothing can ever prepare you for that moment when your parents die, regardless of the nature of your relationship beforehand. Perhaps my grandparents brought into that heartless theory and allowed themselves to be persuaded that it was the best thing for Uncle Frank. So, as was the case in 2010, when the council wanted to ship Steven off to Wales, in 1955, Uncle Frank was decanted from Southall to Derby.

Uncle Frank was one of the first residents when the Staunton Harold home opened in 1955. I have a photo of Leonard Cheshire giving an address from the vestibule at the grand opening, and my Granddad Henry is clearly visible in the crowd on the lawn. Up to that point, Cheshire homes had concentrated on being places for the war wounded or for ex-servicemen who had fallen on hard times. Learning disability hadn't been on their radar before and in the records from the early years, a person's learning disability doesn't get a mention. By 1955, the organisation's reputation was soaring. When you read the transcript of Leonard Cheshire's speech at the grand opening, he comes across as sincere and well meaning, and typical of a certain type of philanthropist whose inclination was to give something back.

In 1955, institutions were not thought of as institutions. There weren't the negative connotations attached to such vast, congregate living places, as there is in the 21st century. Like the deaf school in Margate, the ethos was worthy and the regime was heavily built around encouraging self-sufficiency. And fresh air. As workhouse children in the 19th century were sent away from London to receive the benefits of fresh air, the Leonard Cheshire homes promoted their geographical location and extolled the value of clean air. There was no condition, or ailment, that fresh air couldn't work wonders on. In 2020, it is easy to mock such values, but they were heartfelt and, who knows, they may have worked. Southall was hardly an industrial town, but the fresher air of the Derbyshire countryside may have been beneficial for Uncle Frank. Old fashioned though it may seem nowadays, I refuse to knock the home. It had the typical workshops that you would expect to find in this kind of establishment. Carpentry and metalwork were very popular. But Staunton Harold also encouraged the president's cultural development too. I came across a marvellous photo from around Uncle Frank's time where the residents put on a performance of 'A Midsummer's Night Dream'. There was a fabulously stocked library and learning to play music was high on the daily agenda. When the 2020 idea of support is to take the person window shopping around the precinct, Cheshire must have been considered quite revolutionary. There is something, touchingly quaint about their celebrity supporters who ranged from Dame Sybil Thorndike to Hughie Green.

Was Uncle Frank happy there? Who knows? It must have been a shock to him, having lived as part of a large family with seven siblings within a small, close community for thirty eight years, to be moved halfway across the country to live with complete strangers. I don't think contact with his family would have ceased, but it would have fractured.

Frank Neary died, aged forty, in 1957, two years after moving to Derby. If the move was to prepare him for his later life after his parents had gone, he did not have much of a later life, and passed away before them. His death certificate recorded that he died of acute cardiac failure, after acute bronchial failure, so perhaps he had been ill for some time.

Frank may not have fought in any wars. He may not have owned a chain of tailors. He may not have married and produced a Neary heir. But I know how I feel about him in my heart, so on that score alone - Frank Neary, you did leave your mark on this world.

16. Having A Kickabout.

2019.

It's been a few weeks since our trip to Shoalstone Pool and our encounter with William Worley. It feels like it's time to take the camper van out again. I have decided not to try and contrive the swimming trunks aroma experiment again. If it's going to happen, it will happen in it's own time. I am aware though, that I haven't fully heard the message that the universe is trying to send me and if one is to listen to the universe, one needs to get out into it.

I was sitting in my canal-side flat last week, eating a nonchalant digestive, when I noticed some activity on one of the barges, which was moored outside my living room window. In the six years that I have lived here, I have only seen someone emerge from that boat once. It happened on a freezing cold December morning, when a man in a string vest appeared on deck and proceeded to piss over the side of his boat. Relieved of his bladder excess, he refastened his belt and returned inside. I have never seen him since. Last week, it was a woman who popped out. Rather overdressed for a weekday morning, in a plum coloured cocktail frock, she opened the flap and started to call out, "Padraig" in a shrill Texan twang. Her calls got more frantic until, after five minutes, Padraig appeared. He was a jet black, vastly overweight, Staffordshire bull terrier. Padraig jumped onto the boat and followed his mistress inside. I continued my morning chore of dusting the skirting boards, but I couldn't get the name, Padraig, out of my head.

It was whilst attending to the important task of critiquing 'Homes Under The Hammer', that it came back to me. It was Christmas Eve, 1981, and I was working on the reception desk at the Department of Health and Social Security, in Southall. It was the last day of opening, before Christmas and we were due to shut the doors at 1 o'clock. The place had been heaving all morning, but by now, at 12 o'clock, the waiting room had thinned out and the only people still remaining were those who needed an emergency giro. The main door swung open and a man walked in. He looked odd, in that he was shabbily dressed and unshaven, but he had exactly the same expertly cut, bleached blonde wedge haircut that I had also had styled, especially for the season. He didn't look much older than me and with our matching peroxide barnets, we could have been mistaken for the two brothers from Modern Romance. He approached my booth and I affected my best, customer care greeting.

"Good morning, Sir. Compliments of the season. May I have your name, please?"

"Padraig."

"Thank you. And what's your surname?"

"I don't have one."

"Sorry? You don't have a second name?"

"No. Everyone just calls me Padraig." (This was pre Morse).

And that was as far as he went, namewise. He too wanted an emergency giro. His back story was that he had been invited from Ireland to spend Christmas with a friend. Unfortunately, the friend had given him the wrong address and now he was stuck, with nowhere to go and with no money. I had been working on the main counter for about nine months, so I had heard tall stories like this before. I don't know whether it was his age, or our matching haircuts, but my instinct was to help this guy. My supervisor was having none of this and told me to send him away with a flea in his ear. After much toing and froing and with Padraig swinging between charm and threats, I gave in and gave him £20 from my own pocket. He clearly wanted more, but the security guard had arrived to lock up. Padraig came forward towards me and kissed the anti attack screen that separated us. I wished him well and hoped that he got back safely to Ireland.

An hour later, those of us civil servants who had already done their Christmas shopping and didn't have seasonal sprouts to prepare, were having a jolly drink in The White Swan. Toyah was on the jukebox, and my two bestest mates, the two Sues were giving a formidable rendition of 'It's A Mystery'. It was my round and as I tried to get myself noticed at the bar, someone elbowed me in the ribs as he tried to queue jump. I didn't recognise him at first. He was clean shaven and suited and booted in an excellent tonic suit, just like Chas Smash had worn on last night's 'Top Of The Pops'. I had been admiring the very same suit in the window of Edgar's Modes and had earmarked it for my January pay packet. Another poke in the ribs and then the penny dropped. It was Padraig. He caught the barmaid's eye immediately and ordered a Guinness and a Cinzano Bianco for the stunning redhead who was gripping onto his waistband.

"Padraig. I didn't expect to see you......"

"You, stupid, gullible cunt." He laughed, as he pulled out a wad of notes from his pocket to pay the barmaid and then launched into a full blown snog with the redhead.

That was Christmas finished for me. Jackie had joined the two Sues and they were now giving it large to 'I'm In The Mood For Dancing'. Padraig was cadging a cigarette off my manager. I made an excuse about having to pick up some last minute perishables and slipped away.

Back in 2019 and I so fancy a Cinzano Bianco in The White Swan, Southall. I'm not sure whether you can still buy Cinzano Bianco, but I will settle for nothing less.

It has been years since I've been through Southall and I had forgotten how dreadful the traffic on the High Street can be. I took Steven, Francis and Des along for the ride and it had taken us an hour to get along the Broadway and we were stuck forever on Station Bridge. Steven was getting restless in the camper van. We had put together a "travelling" compilation tape, but there are only so many times that you can listen to 'King Of The Road', before the novelty wears off. Never mind. Our destination was in sight and I could see Regina Road and The White Swan in the distance. Now all we had to do was to find somewhere to park.

We were almost halfway down Clifton Road, when I noticed that something has changed. Underfoot, the road surface felt a lot less smooth. The van was juddering along and it felt like the road hadn't been tarmacked. I glanced out of the window and saw the sign for Pearson's Outfitters. I used to get my school uniforms from there, fifty years ago. I could have sworn that the place closed down, several years ago. By now, I was more than distracted. More people, than is fashionable, were wearing cloth caps. Our turquoise camper van was attracting a lot of attention. The baby buggies had turned into bone shaking prams. A paper boy, in a cloth cap, was whistling, 'You're The Tops'. All the brown faced pedestrians had turned white.

To our right, on the corner of Lea Road, I could see Cooper's General Store. I had been in there many times to buy a Jubbly, whenever we visited Auntie Phil. I asked Des to jump out and buy Steven a packet of crisps, to ward off the sensory overload of the journey. And to pick up a newspaper whilst he's there.

Des seemed a trifle ruffled on his return. He explained that the shop didn't sell crisps, but the shopkeeper was very keen for him to try the newly launched chocolate bar, that had just been delivered that morning. An Aero. Des passed me the newspaper. It was dated 3rd March 1930.

As casually as befits a band of troubled, weary travellers, we parked up outside number 18 Lea Road and I knocked on the door. A woman in her forties answered. She had just had a shampoo and set done and was wearing a lovely, gay pinny. It was my Nan, Annie.

"Mark! Steven! Come on in. Go into the front room with Frank. I'll put the kettle on. Henry will be home in a few minutes."

She gave us both a sloppy, wet kiss and ushered us into the front parlour. A boy of about twelve or thirteen was sitting at the dining table, doing something with some cables. He was deeply immersed and didn't look up. Steven goes to shake his hand.

"Hello, Uncle Frank."

Not looking at him, Frank muttered,

"Where's your manners, Frank Neary? Here they are. Hello, Steven Neary."

This was going to be tricky. Steven doesn't get on too well with other learning disabled people and Frank was deep in concentration with his cables. Steven had finished his Aero and was looking for engagement.

As luck would have it, I glanced out of the window and saw my grandfather wheeling his bike up the garden path. He had died when I was eight months old, so I have no memories of him, but I could see the man, albeit much younger, from the Leonard Cheshire photo. I could hear his key, turn in the front door.

"Hello, my darling. Got the kettle on, Annie?"

"Brew's coming, Henry. We've got visitors."

The friendly faced, prematurely grey, tall man opened the parlour door and his smile lit up the room.

"Well, I'll go the foot of our stairs. You were the last people I expected to see today. Good afternoon, Steven. How are you, old chum?"

"I'm fine. Hello, great grandfather Henry."

He knew!

"Do you want to come into the garden, Steven, and see my birds? Let your Dad have a gossip with his nan."

Steven was off like a shot. He loves going to see his Uncle Wayne's birds, so this was an invitation to heaven. I signalled to the support workers to go with them leaving me on my own with Uncle Frank.

I thought about frequencies. It seemed apt with all the cables about. I had no idea what to say, but made a couple of hideous observations that got no response. Uncle Frank hadn't looked up once since we walked into the room.

Thankfully, my Nan pushed open the door, carrying a tray of tea things. Another kiss and we sat down. I had hundreds of questions to ask, but she was more interested in talking about me and Steven. I felt guilty as I rambled on about the trivia of our life, but she seemed that she genuinely wanted to know. Of course, my burning question was to ask her about Uncle Frank's move to Derbyshire, but I had to remind myself that we had arrived in 1930 and it would be another 25 years before Frank's move. I found myself staring at Uncle Frank and I realised that I was trying to locate a similarity with Steven, when he was the same age. Autism hadn't been invented as a diagnosis in the 1930s, but Frank's almost obsessive attention to detail with his wires had an aching familiarity about it. I thought back to the many hours of observing Steven with his 100s of Playmobile figures out on the mat. No words were ever spoken. Something very intricate and involved was taking place, but we were never party to the operation.

I was being force fed homemade scones, when Steven, my Granddad and the support workers rejoined us. I didn't notice at first, but they've been followed by a small toddler, carrying a football. He kicked the ball towards me a few times and I made him laugh with my over elaborate goal keeping performance. Before we knew it, we were all having a full scale kickabout in my Nan's front-room.

For the first time since we arrived, Uncle Frank looked up from his task and spoke.

"Johnny. Where are your manners? Say hello to Mark."

And I realised that I was playing football with my two-year-old Dad.

17. Love in Thorpe Mews

Sunday afternoons in Kensington in 1908 could be tedious affairs when you are nineteen. Annie Culley had just managed to escape the house and was setting off for a little stroll. It would be an aimless stroll though. There was nobody she especially wanted to visit. In fact, she wasn't sure if she wanted any company at all.

Annie had spent the morning, helping her mother to clean the house and two hours of leading the grate would be enough to dampen anyone's spirits. And it was all so jolly unfair. Her mother never expected her brother to do any of these weekly chores. Her mother argued that the chores were a good rehearsal for "the big day". Annie was shocked when her mother explained that "the big day" meant the time when Annie would be married and it would be her marital duty to black lead her own grate. Annie believed that there was no difference between herself and her brother, William junior. They both worked all week. Why should William get such a cosy ride at weekends, compared to her?

Unfortunately, Annie knew the answer to that question. Her mother was frightened. It had been eight years since her father had been killed in that beastly war in Africa and Annie wasn't sure whether her mother had fully recovered herself, even to this day. And then, a few months ago, William had arrived home after lying that he had been at work and announced that he had enlisted in the Royal Military Corps. Annie watched as all the colour drained out of her mother's face and although William was still waiting for his first posting, Annie could see that there was no respite to her mother's worries. The harsh truth was that Annie knew that she had to be the strong, dutiful daughter if her mother's nerves were not to get the better of her.

Lost in these thoughts, Annie didn't notice that she was approaching that dangerous pothole at the top of Thorpe Mews.

"Damn you, William Culley. I hope you get sent to the Colonies."

Annie heard someone laugh. It was a throaty, deep laugh and she couldn't be sure that her petulant outburst wasn't the cause of the man's amusement. She had been lost in her little world of rants and jealousies and hadn't noticed that she had very nearly stumbled into the pesky crater. She was at the corner of Thorpe Mews. It had been a marvellous blessing when her aunt and her cousin had moved to Kensington. Just five minutes' walk from her own home, spending time with cousin Beatrice offered Annie a merciful release from her choking existence. Whilst Annie was impaired with shyness, Beatrice was a sociable girl who refused to wear the invisible chains like so many of her peers. Even Annie's mother had been alert enough to observe, "Since you've chummed up with Beatrice, you've really come out of yourself." This irritated Annie. She had never really been inside of herself. It was the constraints that her mother put on her that were so terribly limiting.

"Talking to yourself, are you, Miss?"

Annie had turned the corner into Thorpe Mews and almost collided head on, with the man who found her exasperation so amusing. Annie recognised him immediately. He was the son of one of the coachmen, who worked for one of the rich families in Thorpe Crescent. He was much older than most of the young men and boys who spent their spare time loitering around the cabs. Today, he was wearing only a vest above his waist and Annie was careful to avert her gaze. She was already aware that she might be blushing. Despite looking away, Annie had already seen enough to know that he must have been older than twenty to become as thick set as that. In spite of herself, she was enjoying the brief attention of this older man.

"It's Annie, isn't it? Billy Culley's sister? He used to play for our football team down the park. That was before he got big ideas about the army. Has he been given his posting yet?"

"Not yet. I think he is getting a little restless."

"Fool. He ought to count his blessings."

Annie was perplexed. She felt that she should defend her brother's character from the criticism of a complete stranger, but in her heart of hearts, she agreed with every word he said. Her response felt half-hearted.

"He wants to be like his father. Our father served his King and country."

"Lots of ways you can serve your King, without getting yourself killed. My old man drove one of the Princesses back to Buck Palace a few months ago. That's service. My name is Henry Neary, by the way."

"It's very nice to meet you, Henry. I have seen you around. Isn't it a bit chilly to be wearing just your....."

Henry laughed out loud again. Annie could feel her blush returning.

"Well, you're not backwards in coming forwards, are you? I like that in a girl. I'm painting my old man's wheel trims and I didn't want to get paint on my best, Sunday shirt. Hey, guess what? I've got a hot date later."

Anne turned crimson. He doesn't sound offended but had she spoken out of turn? A man's attire was his own business. She was of half a mind to turn around and dash, straight home.

"Don't you want to know who I'm going on a date with?"

"Not really. I don't think that it's my place to ask....."

"You, my little chick. I'm going on a hot date with you. Do you fancy a walk through Kensington Gardens? It's Sunday. There might be a band playing."

And as coolly as you like, Henry washed his hands with a pail and a cloth, slipped his best Sunday shirt back on, threaded his arm through Annie's and led her off in the direction of the park. All before Annie had a chance to answer.

Annie enjoyed her time with Henry immensely. The band were playing and she could see that he was impressed when she told him that she could play both the piano and the trombone. There was an awkward moment when Annie spotted cousin Beatrice taking a short cut, across the lawns. Just once, she implored Beatrice not to notice her. She didn't. And Annie rewarded her own good fortune, by resting her head on Henry's broad shoulder. This fleeting moment of joy made all the black leading, worthwhile.

Fifteen months later, on the 6th December 1909, Henry Neary and Annie Culley were married at the little chapel, hidden behind the primrose trees at Notting Hill. Henry's parents had been the life and soul of the party at the reception, making up hilarious songs about whirlwind romances. Annie found their company and the tunes, highly amusing and they provided some compensation for the sight of her tearful mother, who was trying to make herself invisible by the ladies' powder room. Her brother, William, was absent having been posted to Burma the previous spring. Annie was grateful that her new in-laws were so cheerful and accepting of her, into the family. The jokes were a little near the knuckle and Henry received a fair amount of ribbing, on account of him being ten years older than his new bride.

"Oi, Henry. Thought the old arrow might never get fired before you took to your grave."

Henry took all the mocking in good spirit. And why not? He had found the loveliest girl in the whole of London town. She had goodness, running through her veins. The wedding night beckoned and he couldn't be happier.

For Annie, there was one small cloud that loomed over their perfect day. Following his promotion at work, Henry had been transferred to Paddington Station and the railway had found them a little two-up, two-down. It was in a place, out west, called Southall. The cloud was that Annie had yet to break the news to her mother. How would she cope with both her children leaving home, in the space of four months.

July 1911. West End Road, Southall.

A most remarkable thing had just happened. Annie had taken little Binnie to see Annie's mother. It was quite a turnaround. Annie's mother was positively cheerful. Shortly after the wedding, Mary Culley had given up the house in Kensington. She told her friends that it had become too big for one. She had moved to Paddington. Even more incredulously, Mary had taken over the running of a respectable boarding house. Coincidentally, the lodging house was two minutes walk from Paddington station and every Tuesday, Henry had taken on calling on his mother in law for lunch. After his first visit, he reported back to Annie:

"Your old lady has bounced back, in fine style. It's like a different woman. And she's got all sorts living with her. A right old motley crew. And on the throne, sits your mother. Queen of her very own castle."

This, Annie had to see. Whilst Annie wanted to use the visit to show off her little Binnie, walking her first steps, her curiosity about her mother's new temperament needed to be satisfied. But her mother showed little interest in little Binnie. Instead, she turned the tables and made quite a performance of introducing all the lodgers. There were the three law students: Mr Parkash, Mr Singh and Miss Nath Bose; the two electricians, the two Mr Chesher brothers; and the two widows of private means, Mrs Atkinson and Mrs Partridge. Mary Culley had been in her element. She had served up a sumptuous tea and gave a striking impersonation of the Lady of the Manor as she manoeuvred Annie round the room to engage in small talk with the repertory company of residents.

"Mr Parkash. This is my daughter, Annie. Please tell her your wonderful story about the open-air prayer meetings during the monsoon season. Oh Annie, Mr Om Parkash is a real hoot."

It was all rather theatrical, but Annie was genuinely delighted to see her mother, so content.

Annie changed Binnie and left her to play. She could hear the noise coming from the back yard. She wanted to joke with Henry about the hotchpotch of lodgers, but Henry had been so sullen of late, she was loathe to disturb him. Annie suddenly felt very tired. She sat down and patted her bump, drifting off into a pleasing imagining that it would be nice if it were to be a little brother for Binnie to play with. Annie's dreaming was cut short by a delivery from the postman.

By the time that she returned to the parlour, Annie had opened and read the letter. She was confused and called Henry in from the garden. He had been building a cot for the new baby, and when Henry appeared, Annie could see that he looked more relaxed than he had for several weeks. Since the start of the railway strike, Henry had been morose and distant. Annie passed her husband, the letter.

"It's from the Railway. I don't understand it. What is it saying you have done?"

Henry read the letter and his countenance changed. He screwed the letter into a ball and threw it at the wall.

"It's nothing, Chick. They're bastards. That's all."

Annie retrieved the letter and flattened it out.

"It says they've terminated your contract because you......'interfered with the company's team, during the strike.' What does it mean?"

"Bloody blacklegs. The company brought them in to keep the Paddington to Slough line running. Me and a couple of the lads decided we'd stop them"

"How? What did you do? Don't tell me someone got hurt?"

"What do you take me for, Annie?"

"I don't know, Henry. What did you do?"

"We sat down on the tracks."

It was said, so matter of factly, Annie nearly found it comical. She almost laughed, but she was worried and angry, at the same time.

"You could have been killed. History repeating itself like my father. Do all men have to die for a cause? Do they all have to be bloody heroes? A dead hero and then where would he have been? Me, and Binnie, and this little one in here?"

"We weren't in any danger, Annie. I ain't no hero. There were no trains running as the coal had been delayed."

Henry sat down next to Annie.

"The union are onto it, for us. We'll be taken back on, within the week. Sometimes, Chick, you have to stand up for what is right. Or sit down, as we did."

This time, Annie really did give in to the giggles.

"You'll be the death of me, Henry Neary."

"My old man used to tell me stories of when he was in Jamaica. He became great pals with a man called Victor. This old Victor had been a slave. He fought for years to be a free man. And in the end, he was. He stood up. These days it's different. The bosses have got too much power. We have to fight back. It's not just for us. They're striking in Liverpool and Wales too."

Annie loved this man. She was worried sick, but she couldn't argue with his beliefs.

"Your father died in the Boer, to make the world a better place didn't he? I may not have a rifle, or a pair of pigeons, but that's all I'm trying to do."

Annie got up.

"The pie should be ready. I'll put the veg on."

Reginald Henry Neary was born the following January. Henry Neary missed the birth. He was carrying out repairs on the Paddington to Oxford line.

18. A Cheese Sandwich & A Cuppa

September 2019

It's been a good day. It's been a bloody good day. But this train ride home has been taking forever and I just want to slip out of these sensible trousers and eat a box of Jaffa Cakes.

I've been to Nottingham to tell the Get Steven Home story at a Mental Capacity Act conference. The other speaker was Justice Peter Jackson. Yes, him. The man who saved Steven's life, eight years ago. It feels like many lives have been lived since that day in his courtroom, when he described me as "an unusual man" and caused me to sob, uncontrollably by linking our case to the Magna Carta. What do you say to one of your heroes? I've got form on this. Back in 1980, Southall Football Club's midfield playmaker, started work in the same office as me and we sat at adjoining desks. We were the same age, but it took me days before I could even acknowledge his presence. Once I dealt with my awe, we became good mates. A couple of years later, he arranged a match between our office and Ealing DHSS at Southall's old Western Road ground. Even though I was the worst player in the team, he threw me the match ball and insisted that I led the team onto the pitch. My hero. My mate.

But Justice Peter Jackson was a whole different kettle of fish. It turned out that I was his warm-up man. He was booked to speak after me and was travelling up from London on the morning. That prompted an additional anxiety. Supposing he arrived in the room at the end of my talk? When I got to the bit where I was talking about him? Was Nottingham prepared for a love fest?

After my talk, there was a coffee break and I went outside to collect my thoughts. The venue was an old school, hauntingly reminiscent of my junior school. Apart from the Mental Capacity group, the place was deserted and the eerie corridors felt populated by ghostly kids from my generation. Kids sucking on sherbet lemons. Globes with too much pink on. I got lost, and it was whilst I was walking along one of the silent passages, that the door of the gentlemen's opened and there he was. We shook hands and stood talking on a stairwell for ages, until someone came to find him to start his talk. Justice Jackson went down a storm. He spoke about his job as a decision maker and about being bold and brave. He talked about some of his famous cases and the humanity of the man was powerfully moving.

There are two conversations that I've had in my life, which I will take to my grave. The first was with my Dad, that day in the hospital when he had just been told that he only had a few weeks to live. The second was that day in Nottingham. Justice Jackson and I talked about Steven, of course. And me, and how our lives had changed forever on account of his ruling. We also talked about family, and courage, and where it comes from. And possibly, it was the day that the seeds of this book were planted. One of the delegates appeared and wanted to take a selfie of the three of us. I think that I upset her by declining, but I didn't want that special moment diluted by being turned into an Instagram boast. I have the photo in my head, and my heart, anyway.

All the way home on the train, I was struck by how the encounter had turned out to be, nothing more than just two men, having a chat. No pedestals. I was in awe of him, of course, but I didn't become tongue-tied. We had been in a school, but I hadn't been a little boy. It had taken a long time.

It was nearly 11 o'clock before I turned the keys in my flat. I might even give the Jaffa Cakes a miss and go straight to bed. I switched on the hall lights and got a peculiar sensation, like I was back in the deserted school, from this morning. It had been raining buckets and I went into the bathroom to dry off. Being a Yul Brynner lookalike, rainwater tends to just sit on my head, but as I dried my head in the dark, I could feel hair. I switched on the bathroom light and a man with my face, my wrinkles, my liver spots, looked back at me from the mirror. Only, he had a feather cut and little droplets of rain fell from it and into the sink. I went into the bedroom, to slip into something more comfortable. I could feel the muscles that I had been so painstakingly cultivating. I could feel the foot long scar from my recent cancer operation. But outside of them, I could see a pair of high-waisted flared trousers and one of my Auntie Hilda's hand-knitted tank tops. A wolfman in Leo Sayer clothing.

This was all, rather weird. I must be tripping. I thought that the two lads, standing next to me at the bus stop, outside Uxbridge Station, had been smoking a joint. Was that why I'd developed an insatiable appetite for Jaffa cakes?

I went into the living room. Everything looked just as I had left it, yesterday morning. I phoned Steven for a quick chat about The Pet Shop Boys and Maltesers, and then switched on the radio. The disc jockey sounded remarkably like Emperor

Rosco. "And this week's number one is Abba. It's Mama Mia." And Agnetha and Frida started singing about being cheated on from a time that they couldn't quite put their fingers on.

I walked across to the kitchen. I put the washing up away. Next to the draining board, was a side plate with a grated cheese sandwich on. And a cup of tea. And the cup of tea had steam coming off it.

I turned around abruptly. There she was, sitting in my armchair. My Mum. My legs went wobbly. I kept looking back and forth from the radio to her. "This week's number one!" February 1976. The month and the year that she died.

"Is it you? Shit. Is it really you?"

"Mark. Of course, it's me. Who were you expecting? Gina Lolabrigita?"

"I dunno. Oh my. It's bloody good to see you."

"It's been forty-three years."

I look back over to the radio. I'm trying to process forty-three years. Abba faded into a commercial break. I switched the radio off and collapsed onto the sofa. I didn't know what to say.

"Mama Mia. It was number one, the week that you died. I underlined it five times in my red It book."

"I know. I went too soon. I never got to hear Fernando."

She was making a joke. She was making a bloody joke.

"You didn't miss much. Although, Dancing Queen was a classic and has really stood the test of time."

Our first conversation in forty three years and we're discussing Abba.

"Your tea is getting cold. Steven had a great time at his water aerobics group today. He doesn't miss you at all when you go away. God, I'm proud of him."

Mechanically, I sip my cuppa.

"Me too. Look, please say, if this is too much to ask... What was...Bugger... what was 1976 like? For you?"

This is coming out all wrong.

"I'm not sure that there's too much to say. I ended. When you're dead, your life has stopped. That's the end of the story. Well, the end of my story. Only the living can tell their story."

"You can tell it now. It would be good to hear."

"That Justice Jackson is a nice man, isn't he. Well spoken. And a cheeky glint in his eye. Reminds me of old Mr Tipper. Do you remember him?"

"Yes, of course. He taught me everything I know about slicing a quarter of a pound of tongue."

"He always used to slip an extra slice of corned beef into my order. And then he winked."

We both laughed. I didn't know how long we had together. She didn't want to talk about the end. I don't blame her really.

"You're having quite an adventure. I've learned such a lot about the Worleys. And my mother was always very quiet about the Fleetwoods. We never understood that when we were growing up, but you've helped me get more of a handle on it."

"That seems to be a common theme through several generations of our family. The stories and the lives that were never spoken about. There are a lot of stories that I was never told. Uncle Frank. How the Farwells got bombed to death during the war. What happened to Granddad Worley. Lots of stories. Why don't I know about any of those?"

Mum joined me on the sofa. For the first time, I noticed her familiar smell. I'd forgotten how comforting it was. She smiled.

"You've always had an arrogant streak in you. Do you remember that time when you organised a sports day in the back garden and Uncle Albert won the sack race? You were devastated because you'd assumed that you would win."

I squirmed. She had always been good at telling someone a few home truths, without slicing off their balls in the process. Twitter could learn a lot from her.

"Do you tell people what your Dad said to you, that day in hospital? Do you talk about losing your baby? You've been very quiet about how losing me has affected your relationship with women."

"Yeah. Don't rub it in. I get the point. I probably won't tell anyone about what's happening right now....."

"Of course you will. Because it won't hurt you. For someone who counsels others, you can be pretty thick at times. What happened to the Farwells was a life changing tragedy. Six people, here one day, and gone, the next. You can't blame Albert Farwell for burying that one away. Besides, he's not going to talk about it in the middle of the conga, on New Year's Eve."

I shift my position a bit closer. I'm not sure whether it's appropriate to request a hug from a ghost.

"Okay. I get all that. But what about Uncle Frank? This whole journey started with him. Why was he erased from the family memoir?"

"There you go again. Just because you didn't know him, you've assumed nobody cared."

I don't like the feeling, but I'm starting to feel pissed off. That's no answer at all. I think Mum reads my mind.

"Sorry. You're right. I'm being unfair. In the space of five years, your Dad lost his three brothers. Reggie never recovered from the war and took himself away from his family. He must have been in torment. Stan emigrated to

Australia. John really looked up to him. And I don't think the family ever got over the guilt of losing Frank. They thought he was going away to a better life."

Bloody hell, these trousers feel tight. I look down at my lap and I'm back in my sensible trousers. The flares have gone. I touch my head. All I can feel is skin. Mum appears to have noticed this.

"A bald head suits you. Let's the world see your toughness. It goes well with your kind eyes."

I haven't really looked at her, until now. She looks the same as the picture that I've kept in my head for all these years. I am sixty. She is forty two. How does that work?

"You must understand their guilt? Do you ever feel it? With Steven?"

"Yep. I just try to do my best."

"The 1950s were a different world. You were right about that home Frank went to. They tried to do their best too. For a while, everyone thought it was for the best. Until he became ill. That's when you need your family. He wasn't exactly round the corner where we could just pop in"

"When I was in hospital, Jayne and Wayne came every day. Carol came too. And all the support workers came too. They're family."

"We were all there. Just like everyone was there for me in 1976. It's called family. You need love and bravery to watch the people you care about the most, dying."

We slip into silence. I reckon saying 'goodbye' requires balls whether you are there or not. We all find our own way. Dad's brothers all said their goodbyes in different ways. Painful ways for them and for the people who loved them. I still feel uneasy that, unlike the others, Uncle Frank didn't have a choice, but that has always been the way for people with learning disabilities. It'll be the same for Steven.

"I'll tell you what I like about my job. People think counselling is all about asking questions. It's not. It's two people, in a room, hanging out together. Talking about shit that matters."

"I've seen some of your sessions. I don't know how you get away with charging people £30 to sit in a room for an hour, talking about Morse."

I splutter my tea all over the carpet. We both fall about laughing.

"Sorry about Julie, by the way. Hanging out, you say? I was looking at your DVD collection before you got home. There's hardly anything that I know. Do you know what? I quite fancy putting my feet up on the sofa and watching something. Just hanging out. If you're not too tired?"

I go across to the shelf unit that holds the pride of my living room.

"I've got 'Crossroads'. The best of Crossroads. It's got the episode when Meg remarried. And Larry Grayson played her chauffeur."

"Ooh. Shut that door, Everard."

"And then the really sad episode where Meg left for the last time on the QE2."

"That one was after my time."

"Oh yes, of course. Noelle Gordon died soon after. It's a good one though. I'll open the Jaffa Cakes. Do you want one? Help yourself to as many as you want, whilst I go and change out of these bloody trousers."

The familiar theme tune fills the room. Sandy appears in the motel lobby, in his wheelchair. Vince, the postman, arrives with the mail. I look across at Mum and speculate that if she had died twenty years later, we might be watching an episode of 'Gladiators' now and I could invite her grandson round to provide a running commentary.

She looks content. Just hanging out.

19. Tom

2018.

Boy, am I cheesed off. This is the fourth day of jury service and we haven't set foot inside the courtroom yet. We haven't been told anything about the case, or even if there is a case, but the whisper is, three of the prosecution witnesses have gone missing. The judge is prepared to give the players one more twenty-four hour deadline, before halting the trial. At least today we won't be sitting around like lemons. We have been dismissed for the day and it is still only ten thirty. For the last three days, I have been trapped in the jury room, with nothing more than a few gardening magazines for entertainment. So I've been occupying myself by playing the world's least imaginative game - where would you rather be, than here? Today, I have the chance to jump onto the train and get back home before Loose Women, but I have suddenly discovered a fancy to explore the delights of Brentford. My sole experiences of Brentford this week have been the station, the greasy spoon caff, and the County Court. Surely, Brentford has more to offer a yokel from Cowley. I have taken out one of those go-anywhere gym passes. It has been over a week since I last did a legs workout and, in my fragile bodybuilder's eyes, my quads are shrinking fast.

I leave the courthouse and punch the postcode of the gym into Google Directions. I was a useless navigator when all we had was paper Ordnance Survey maps and I'm no better trying to read the Google version. I can see where I am and I can see where I want to be, but unless the instructions begin from the exact same paving stone that I'm standing on, I'm flummoxed. There is no point in telling me to walk four hundred yards and then to turn left into Flummoxed Street, when I can't work out in which direction I have to walk those four hundred yards. Still, it is good to be out in the fresh air and I convince myself that the walk will be a good warm up for my hams.

Twenty five minutes later and Google is informing me that I am 1.3 miles from my desired destination. This is a pisser, because I was only 0.5 miles away when I started. It is hot and I am wearing my favourite two-tone suit. In this heat, my armpits are beginning to develop a patch. I am aware that I haven't passed a station during my constitutional and I have started to consider giving up and going home; even if I stop off somewhere for brunch, I can still make it back to my own gym in Cowley by 2 o'clock. In the distance, I can vaguely make out a roadsign bearing a name from the past. Kew Gardens. Back in my DHSS days, I spent a month on a training course at Kew. Every day for four weeks, I set my alarm for 5.30, caught the 65 bus from Ealing Broadway and lost myself during the meandering bus journey in speculations about the horticultural treasures behind the high walls of the Garden's boundaries. For that whole month, I never alighted the 65 to discover what lay behind those brick defences. How about I make today that day? The only problem is that the River Thames separates me from it. Like a man with a mission, I step up my pace and head on down towards the river. Perhaps my mission is to locate a bridge. I'm pretty sure that once I'm across the river and sated by Kew's finest blooms, my historical radar will lead me to a number 65 bus stop to return home. I am almost at the river's edge.

There is a God. I spy, with my little eye, a pub with a sign outside advertising all-day breakfasts. I increase my step. I con myself that I can burn off the fry-up in the gym and then restrict myself to a couple of whey-protein shakes for the rest of the day. I stand in the car park of the Brewery Tap and my eyes light up when I see that they have fried bread on offer as part of the Bargeman's Bonanza Breakfast. No worries. An extra set of squats and five minutes of abdominal crunches should sweat away a single fried slice.

No way! The pub is closed for refurbishment. It reopens on 8th September, which adds salt to my wound because that is the day that I go into hospital for my preliminary cancer surgery. See Naples and die? See Brentford and starve.

With nowhere else to go, I turn left onto the Brent towpath and head downstream. If I can find the Thames, I might be able to find myself. Perhaps a swim across the Thames will dull my appetite. As well as having a hopeless sense of direction, my sense of distance is pretty poor too. As I stand on the edge of the water, I cannot get any sense at all of the distance to the other side. I'm as lost in furlongs and fathoms as I am in kilometres. Not that I am seriously planning to swim. If nothing else, I don't want to get the Inspector Morse novel in my jacket pocket soaking wet.

I think about Auntie Hilda and that day we lost our bearings in Weymouth:

"Let's just have a nice little sit and see in which direction, the seagulls are heading."

I didn't understand that forty-five years ago and I still don't today. I gaze around for some seagulls, but all I can see are a couple of pigeons, bracing themselves for some sex.

"You be wanting on going over the river, mate?"

My pigeon voyeurism ends abruptly and I see a tall bloke, in an oil-encrusted canvas smock, standing on top of a barge. I think it is the oldest, most rusty boat I have ever seen. I know about this stuff because I live in a bachelor pad, alongside the canal. I am not sure that this stationary craft would survive moving a foot, let alone get us down the Brent and across the Thames. Yet, and I can't quite put my finger on why, there is something okay about the bargeman. He has the air of being a good man in a crisis.

"I need to get over the river to the Gardens. I fancy taking in some greenery. Seem to remember that I can pick up the 65 bus there."

"Well, you'd better climb on, then. I'm going that way. I've got a few errands to run."

I do climb on. This is so unlike me. In no time, the boatman sets off. The first thing that feels peculiar is that the boat isn't motor driven. He is using an implement that looks like a cross between a punt-pole and a paddle and by crikey, does he quickly build up a head of speed. He is going as fast as we might have done if the boat had an engine. I become fascinated by his dexterity with the oar. It verges on art. And then I see his arms. Huge trunks. I would have to train arms every day and take shedloads of performance enhancing substances, to get even close to that size.

"Get out of the way. Move, you fucking maniac."

A small motor boat has come recklessly close to ours. The guy driving the boat looks coked up to his eyeballs. Despite the danger he is causing, he is finding the game hilariously funny. There is a little boy in the back of the boat. The driver is obviously taunting us. My new mate is struggling to prevent the giant oar from hitting their boat. He has to keep whipping the oar out of the water, which causes our boat to change direction abruptly. On the seventh round of Mr Cokehead's perilous game of water bumper-cars, the inevitable happens. The two boats collide and the small boy falls into the water.

The bargeman passes me the oar.

"Here. Take this. No fancy business. Just keep rowing it in the same direction."

He takes off his top and boots and empties his pockets onto the deck. With the oar in one hand, I try to grab him.

I know who my chauffeur is.

"Thomas! What do you think you are doing? I can't fucking row this thing!"

He didn't hear me. He dives in. The boy has disappeared underwater. His father is going bananas. I can't see Thomas or the boy and I am stuck in the middle of the River fucking Thames. After what feels like forever, Thomas emerges from the brown, muddy water. He is carrying the boy aloft. The boy is out, but Thomas's head keeps disappearing back into the sludgy flow. Surprisingly, they are only a few feet from the barge. In my shock and horror, I haven't attempted a single stroke, but the current must have propelled the boat along.

"Mark! Bring the boat towards me! I can't swim, with the nipper."

I grab the oar as tightly as I can and miraculously, the barge starts moving. Just getting the oar to do one full motion takes all my strength and I vow never to wimp out during a session of arm curls, ever again. In about six strokes, I am close enough for Thomas to be able to touch the boat. I lean forward and take hold of the boy. It hasn't occurred to me that he may be dead and, thankfully, he is breathing. There are a couple of blankets on the deck, so I remove the boy's wet clothes and wrap him in the warm woollens. He is conscious, but obviously cold and in shock, so he doesn't say a word. As I have been preoccupied, I haven't noticed that Thomas has dragged himself out of the water and taken charge of the oar that I carelessly abandoned whilst looking after the boy.

"You did well, mate. And by the way, the name is Tom. People don't call me Thomas."

"Sorry, Tom. You did pretty good yourself, fella."

We are back on the riverbank. A large crowd has gathered. A police officer has handcuffed Mr Cokehead. A woman summoned by the coppers announces herself to be a social worker and takes the boy from my arms. Instinctively, I kiss his head. After mooring the barge, Tom goes up and has a few words with the police officers. Rubberneckers start to disperse to post their footage on Instagram. Two policewomen lead the boy's father to the waiting police van. As quickly as the drama unfolded, it dissipates, leaving just the two of us, sitting on the riverbank. I offer Tom a cigarette, and he takes the longest drag imaginable.

"They said we can go home. They'll be round to take statements later."

"Okay."

I realise that I am trembling. I'm not cold because the sun is still blazing down. I think it is the shock. Tom is trying to wring out his trousers.

"Oh shit, Tom. I'm sorry. I gave both the blankets to the boy."

"Don't worry, mate. I've been in worse situations. I'll dry off."

It is time to go. Tom takes control of the oar and five minutes later, we are heading for the exact spot we started from. I have forgotten all about Kew Gardens and the number 65 bus. We travel the whole width in silence. Tom moors up and we stand on the bank, facing each other, neither of us sure what to say or do next. If only the Brewery Tap wasn't closed. I could murder a pint.

"If you don't mind, Mark, I'll go home now. Need to get something dry on."

He shakes my hand and heads off the same way that I arrived from earlier. He turns back to me, laughing. He is leaning against a bus stop.

"See this? The number 237. It'll take you to Hounslow. You can change there for a bus to Cowley"

The bus stop is about twenty feet from the spot where I had been reading the breakfast menu.

"You knew that all along? Why did you take me out in the boat?"

"You mentioned the 65 from Kew and I fancied a little adventure. It gets mighty boring on the water, these days."

Laughing even louder, he walks off. Goodness knows why as the joke has been at my expense, but I start to laugh too and I know that I have to know, so I run after him.

"Tom! Tom. Stop. How could you do that? I mean, dive into the water, after the kid? How could you do that, after what happened before?"

"Tsk. That was years ago. When you fall off your bike, you get straight back on."

"But you drowned....."

"I drowned because I let my anger get the better of me. For a foolish five minutes, I lost sight of how angry the Thames can be when you don't respect it."

"From what I know, you had every right to be angry. Your livelihood was at stake."

"Bollocks. No job is worth losing your life for. I thought I owned the river. Those lads from the North were only here looking for work. Every man has the right to do that."

"I'm really sorry. You deserved a longer life. My Nan Emma deserved having her father around longer. You did the decent thing. Like today..."

"Nobody got a medal for throwing their toys out of their pram. I broke the rules of the river. I paid my price."

"What a price, though? You were a great lighterman, Tom Fleetwood."

"It's over, all that. It's history. Now, fuck off and go the gym. You'll never be a lighterman with arms like that."

This time, he really does go. I am not ready to catch the bus yet. I clamber back on the barge and light another cigarette. For the first time, I notice the name of the boat. It is the 'Life of Findlay'. Half an hour later and I am ready to move on. It will be quite a story to tell Steven. He is probably the only person that I know who will accept that I have just had the adventure of a lifetime with my great-grandfather

20. Two Men on A Boat

Two men stood on the deck of the *SS Minnetonka* at the Port of London. It was 23rd July, 1913. Shortly, the ship would set sail to Ellis Island, New York: a seven-day voyage and the start of a new life in America. The two men were Henry Daubney, my great uncle; and James Hamlet Daubney, his eighteen-year-old son.

The passage was difficult, but convivial. For the most part, the passengers were treated no better than the cargo. Resentment and envy dripped from every single one of the jealous crew. All the passengers were embarking on a thrilling adventure - a new beginning in the New World and the crew hated them for that. Under normal circumstances, Henry Daubney's Irish blood would have boiled at such treatment and his fists would have been put to good use, but on this voyage, the bitterness of others mattered not one jot. The drink had been plentiful and his anticipation of what lay ahead rendered redundant any displeasure at their treatment from the crew. The same could be said for the younger man, James Hamlet Daubney. He was in good spirits. Cut from the same cloth as his father, he held no truck with men who were consumed by petty jealousies. Besides, he was thoroughly enjoying nautical life. By the evening of the second day aboard, he had successfully persuaded a gorgeous Italian serving maid, who had been flirting outrageously with him at an impromptu below-decks dance, to partner him in a private horizontal hornpipe. What man could fail to feel satisfied at such good fortune?

In the afternoon of the 26th, having tended to their toilet in their third-class cabin, Henry and son were taking some whiskey on the south deck. Henry was composing a short letter to his beloved Elizabeth, whilst James Hamlet had lost himself in daydreams of his new life ahead on Rhode Island. Neither man had noticed the middle-aged couple who had sat down beside them on rickety deckchairs. Only the perfume of some freshly opened Bourbon aroused the interest of Henry. The couple introduced themselves as Mr and Mrs Lionel Archer, from Bournemouth, England. They were travelling to visit their son, Mr Walter Archer, who had settled in America during the exceptionally cold winter of 1909. This was their first trip overseas and today was their first venture outside of their cabin, having finally found their sea legs. Mrs Lionel Archer was a martyr to her digestion and had been left prostrate for three days and three nights. Henry was particularly interested to register the news that the Archers had needed several tumblers of Dutch courage to get them this far. He anticipated a pleasurable, thirst-quenching afternoon ahead. Having read his father's thoughts, James Hamlet smiled and poured each of his new travelling companions several fingers of Ireland's finest. Mrs Lionel Archer affected a display of declining, but James Hamlet knew that she was playing her own little comedy and encouraged the Archers to 'knock it back in one'. The Daubneys burst into a generous round of applause as the Archers succeeded with their challenge and Henry took this opportunity to suggest to Mr Lionel Archer that he share around his bottle of Bourbon. Mr Lionel Archer's response couldn't have been kinder.

Lighting his pipe, James Hamlet felt a sudden splash of water hit his back. He turned around in suspicion, to see the beautiful Italian serving girl waving impishly at him. James Hamlet had never seen a more gorgeous woman. She had a natural, confident, Mediterranean beauty that would have been unheard of in Brentford. He knew that her seniors would not permit her to join in with the passengers' revelry. She had implored him, the night before, to keep their tryst a secret, for fear of instant dismissal. At this moment, James Hamlet was harbouring a hankering for having his horn piped again; and there would be plenty of other occasions during the passage for more communal drunkenness. He formed a plan.

"Father, I fear I may be getting a fever. I wonder whether a short nap in the cabin might revive me? I throw down a challenge to you, Father. I am sure that the superb Archers would be desirous of hearing your tales of your many adventures with Alfred the Great."

"Alfred, the great?" enquired Mrs Lionel Archer.

James Hamlet continued his Pootering performance:

"Not any old Alfred, dear Mrs Lionel. The Alfred to whom I refer is Mr Alfred Gwynne Vanderbilt, one of the richest men in all of America. It is to his palatial home that my father and I are now travelling. He and my father are bosom buddies, from way back."

Mr Archer scoffed:

"The fever and the liquor are unhealthy bedfellows. I swear that this story is a load of old Mrs. Worthington's grouts. Such tosh does not become you, young man."

James Hamlet was offended and this would usually have led to a fist fight, but he could feel a pleasurable anticipation causing growth behind his fly-buttons and he was determined that his father should play along with his diversion.

"Perhaps another miniscule dram to oil my vocal cords," suggested Henry, with a barely concealed wink.

James Hamlet smiled too. He was keenly aware that his father needed no prompting to tell the world about his friendship with the great millionaire and how he had taught the American everything he knew about getting the best out of a carriage-racing horse. James Hamlet would listen attentively for five minutes in a display of loyalty and then quietly slip away to his cabin for some sport of his own.

Henry drained the last of his drink and held out his glass towards Mr Archer for a refill. He gestured to his audience for them to draw their deckchairs closer.

"It was 1899, it was. I had been a groom and carriage-driver for many a year. I had my sweet little Elizabeth at home, looking after the three nippers, as we had at the time. We had Henry junior, young James Hamlet here, and the baby, Claude. When you're a 'orseman, you have to get yourself out and about and that can be hard for the family, back home. Although I was often away for weeks at a time, there was always food on the table. I won't hear any man say otherwise.

It's right simple, you see. You're either good with an 'orse, or you ain't. And I've always had a natural affinity with the 'orses, since I was a little lad. I was better with 'orses than I was with people, as my old mother used to say. And she was right enough. Wouldn't give humans the shit off me shoes. If you tell an 'orse to go left, they'll always go left. If you tell a man or a woman to go left, they's want to know why they're going left. Always got a question or a reason not to do what you're asking. Ain't that right, James Hamlet? James? The bugger's gone off. Can't say that I blame him. He's heard this tale, many a time....

When I were a nipper, my old man worked in the slaughterhouse. Many a day, he took me and my sister, Mary-Jane to work with him. She loved it; got right stuck in. Me, I hated it. I know that some sod has got to do it, but it wasn't my idea of honest work to go about killing animals. I wasn't soft, don't misunderstand me, but I was more interested in what they could do when they were alive. I vowed then, that if I was going to do anything with my life, it would be about bringing out the best in an animal. I quickly learned that it was with 'orses that I could do this best.

Anyway, there I was. One of the best judges of horseflesh in all the land. I had been working as a groom at the Albany. I was the man they called upon whenever an 'orse got a bit uppity. 'Where's Henry? He'll calm the blighter down,' they would say. This particular day, I had been sent to some fox-hunting function, out at Syon House. I was tending to a beautiful, frisky grey, out front, whilst the nobs were having their dinner inside. And all the time that I was working, there was this grand nob, sitting on the grass, not taking his eye off me. I'd be having a little chat with this grey stunner and I'd look back around, and there he was, still watching me out. I was getting a bit narky, as it happened. A man don't want an audience from no stuck-up nob.

So, I calls him out. Asked him what he thought he was looking at. I told him that if he didn't mind his own business, I'd have to assist him to sling his effing hook. And do you know what the flash sod did? He laughed at me. Not a quick laugh that is over in seconds, but a bloody marathon chuckle. I was about to lamp him one, nob or no nob. But then he pulls out this hip flask from his jacket and he pours me a large one. Fills the glass to the brim. Same stuff as this. A healthy drop of Bourbon. So, I'm drinking his drink and thinking that he might not be such a bad sort after all, and he shakes my hand, and says,

'The name is Alfred. And it's a great honour to make your acquaintance.'

He had a funny voice. Deep, but a bit of a twang, like he was plucking a banjo. I asked whether he was from these parts and he said, no, he was from America, which explained the banjo.

Over a couple more bourbons, or five, he tells me that he is looking for a good trainer and after watching me for the past hour, he reckons that he's found the perfect man for the job. I told him to watch his lip, but he said that if he'd learned one thing from his business travels, it was to trust his instinct. And how about it? Was I on board? Was I as good a stableman as he thought? Well, I thought, Mr American nob, you don't have the monopoly on instinct. I'd worked out that he seemed a pretty, decent sort, and looking at the cut of his outfit, there might be a decent bit of money in it for me. So, I said, yes.

That were fourteen years ago and we've been inseparable ever since. Me, the Irish rogue, and him, the Yankee swell. It's him who has paid for this journey. I've done the trip about five times before, but a few months back, we were in the stables and he said,

'Henry, my old mucker. This just won't do, any longer. How about you move out to America? Permanently. Come on your own to begin with, and if you find you can settle, bring the rest of your family out later. I'll cover the fares and the housing for them all. The more the merrier. What do you say, old chap?'

What do you say? I was as keen as mustard, and so was James Hamlet. Where the chuffing hell has he gone? The missus wasn't too sure at first, but she's come round to the idea now. It's my eldest that is full of hesitation. And I worry about my sister. She's a widow woman after her husband drowned in the Thames, but she's got herself a new man, so I think she will be alright. So I said yes and here we are.

All those years. He never said as much, but I swear that he saw me as his right-hand man. I would never let any scoundrel get the better of him, not that he hasn't got the brain to spot a wrong 'un. He spent many of his days in England. He was into his Coaching, as it is called. All the toffs and nobs, in their shiny coaches, haring it down from London Bridge to Brighton. I've seen some sights in those races that would make your hair curl. Of course, he had the money for the best 'orses. Everyone knew Mr Alfred. What with him having the best 'orses and his money and his good looks. He could attract the women, no mistake. I'd never seen a collection of 'orses so fine. Purebreds, every one of them.

216

Magnificent creatures and I had the honour of looking after them. Makes a man real proud when he sees his 'orses and his master, winning by a country mile. Yep. That nob. Alfred Vanderbilt. He's done alright for me and my family."

Henry had been talking for over an hour, during which several more glasses had been drunk. Mrs Lionel Archer fell off her deckchair with a resounding thud. Not many yards away, in one of the *Minnetonka*'s cabins, an eighteen-year-old adventurer let out a yell of immense pleasure.

Three days later, the ship docked at Ellis Island. Two men called Daubney were collected personally by Mr Alfred Vanderbilt and taken to a drinks gathering at his apartment, to celebrate their arrival. From there, sated, and full of soak, father and son retired to their new homes, in America.

Postscript

The Daubneys did settle in America. Two years later, in 1915, Henry's wife, Elizabeth and two of their sons, Claude and Lesley, joined Henry. In 1919, Henry's eldest son, Henry junior, completed the transition of all of Henry senior's sons. Finally, in 1920, Henry junior's wife, Ethel, their three children, children and Ethel's cousin, Annie, braved the journey and now the entire Daubney family were settled in America. James Hamlet married Marjorie in 1916 and they settled and raised their family in Massachusetts.

On 7th May 1915, Alfred Gwynne Vanderbilt was travelling home from England on HMS Lusitania. Just off the coast of Ireland, the ship was torpedoed by a German U Boat. The huge liner sank within twenty minutes. Alfred Vanderbilt was preparing to escape onto a lifeboat, when he noticed a young mother carrying her baby. The woman didn't have a lifejacket, so Alfred gave her his. Alfred Vanderbilt was not one of the survivors. He was 38.

The 1940 American census reveals that Claude Daubney, son of Henry Daubney and the younger brother of James Hamlet, was employed as a butler to the nephew of Alfred Vanderbilt.

Alfred Vanderbilt was responsible for the relocation of twenty-one members of the Daubney family to Rhode Island, America. Four generations later, the Daubney family continues to thrive in the USA.

21. Forty

1999 was a pretty decent year, apart from Cliff Richard's 'Millennium Prayer'. It was the year that I turned forty. I had been a father for five years, but I hadn't focused much on the reality of getting older. I certainly didn't feel middle-aged. It was twenty years on from The Railway Tavern, but I still favoured a sharp-looking tonic suit and Martha Reeves and the Vandellas were never too far away from my turntable.

Big changes were happening in 1999. On my fortieth birthday, on the 24th March, I was seven days away from leaving the job that I had been doing for the previous 12 years as a training manager in a large benefits department at Ealing Council. In December 1998, a private company based in Lancashire had won an outsourcing contract and had taken over the running of the department. They had no interest in training, so offered me a choice of redeployment to their head office in Bolton, or redundancy. With all due respect to that fine Lancashire town, I had no intention of uprooting Julie and Steven, so redundancy it was.

I had loved that job, particularly over the preceding five years. A young, progressive manager had joined the council in the early nineties and encouraged me to concentrate less on the tiresome legislation training that had been my main role and instead, design some courses where the emphasis was on personal and professional development. Some of the old-school managers weren't impressed with this new direction, but I was like the cat that had got the cream. I was in a unique position, with advantages enjoyed by no-one else within the department. I had the responsibility of teaching all the staff, but I wasn't in a role where authority and power can lead to troublesome working relationships. I met people when they were at their best. I knew that I was respected and well-liked by the vast majority of my colleagues. Going to work never felt like a chore and at times, could be quite inspirational.

Yet timing of the redundancy couldn't have been more perfect, because I was in my final year of training to become a counsellor. It hadn't been a planned career change at all. It came about during the personal development courses that I had been running. My mate, Tim, had been in one of the groups and we went for a drink during one lunch break. Extremely casually, he said to me, "You should think about becoming a counsellor, Mark. You've got a gift for getting people to open up and people feel safe with you." That very same evening, I was flicking through the local paper whilst on the bus journey home and spotted an advertisement for the recruitment evening at Uxbridge College. One of the courses being promoted was their Certificate in Counselling course. The recruitment event was that evening, so I did a quick detour on the bus and signed up, there and then. I arrived home, two hours late, to inform my bewildered wife that I had just taken the first step towards a major career change. I told her not to worry, because although I had no idea of the earning potential of a counsellor, I was sure that we would still be able to afford our weekly Sunday roast at The Turk's Head.

In Year Two of the training, I got a student placement at a local counselling agency and was hopeful and reasonably confident that they would offer me a paid position, once I qualified. Ealing Council paid me one whole year's gross salary as my redundancy payout, so I was able to go into my final year of training without the pressure of having to find a new job.

Having what amounted to a gap year in my forties meant that I had plenty of time on my hands outside of the course work and the placement. One of the senior staff at the college took a shine to me and offered me some part-time teaching work there. I did two years of running their 'Training for Trainers' diploma. It was fun, but it wasn't what I wanted to be doing with my life and I needed something else, less academic and less touchy-feely, to do. I hit upon the idea of taking my bodybuilding to another level.

Since my mid-twenties, I had used a bench and some free weights at home and had made some reasonable gains. All my training equipment had been set up in our spare room, but since Steven had come along, the spare room had become his room and my training had become sporadic. It was mainly down to other priorities and the sheer joy of hanging out with Steven, but it was laziness too. I could prop the bench up in our bedroom and drag it onto the landing each time I wanted to use it, but carrying the weights up from the shed every day was too tiresome. By 1999, my motivation was back with a vengeance.

At this time, a UK bodybuilder called Dorian Yates was on an incredible run of success at the Mr Olympia competition and I found reading about his training methods inspirational. I knew that I would never achieve the size that I wanted on our landing, so I joined a gym. I completely underestimated the task ahead. On my first day at the gym, the manager showed me the ropes. I may have bigged up the training I had been doing at home, because as we were doing some lat pulldowns, he exclaimed, "Christ, Mark. You've got no back." He was right. I had been limited by the equipment at home and had never really trained my back. I do thrive on a challenge, though. Over the next few months, I was determined to get those lagging areas to catch up and for the most part, I succeeded. I gave my heart and soul, twice a week, in my back workouts and true enough, my posture changed and I grew a back. The rest of me thickened out, but my weakness, then and for the next 18 years was that I was too casual with my diet. All the good work in the gym was great, but my penchant for a Bakewell tart prevented me from becoming the next Dorian Yates. Even a very brief flirtation with steroids, despite piling on the mass, counted for little, when I would scoff a couple of doughnuts on my way home from the gym. It took me eighteen years to learn a hard lesson and then sodding cancer struck.

Being forty was cool. I loved being a Dad. I knew that I would make a good counsellor. I had well and truly caught the bodybuilding bug. And Cliff Richard was pipped to the Christmas number one by Westlife.

The other good thing about being forty is that you can convince yourself that you've still got more than half of your life left. You can't do that at sixty.

Meanwhile, in 1875, in Kensington, someone else was celebrating their fortieth birthday. James Neary had been discharged from the navy in 1870. He had served for twenty-two years, much longer than he had expected, but being short on ideas of what he wanted to do with the second half of his life, he had repeatedly extended his service.

After many years of silence, word had reached James that his father was in poor health. His mother had died in 1866 and the letter from his aunt had revealed that his father was not expected to see another summer. James thought about Harrow and his time working in the shop. His aunt's letter indicated that the brotherly wrangling over the business had finally been settled. His eldest brother, George, had flown the white flag and purchased a shop of his own, further along the High Street. His youngest brother, Henry, had also pulled out of the fight and moved to Birmingham with his new wife, where he was in the process of building his own Midlands grocery empire. William Neary had been the victor. Quiet, unassuming, life-long bachelor William, who had devoted his entire adult life to being his father's second in command, was now First Admiral of the Neary family business and most probably would be sole owner of the grocer's shop after his father passed away. Having been absent from the shop for many years, James couldn't feel bitter or hurt that there was no place for him at the grocer's; he was not in the least inclined to return to his former life. "Good on them all," was his genuine reaction. He knew that, for him, Harrow would remain consigned to history. Yet the letter turned his thoughts towards life after the end of his seafaring days.

Then one day in 1869, he woke up aboard ship with a very clear idea of what he wanted to achieve from life ashore. A wife and family were certainly top of his list. Secondly, a job that came with its own accommodation, like he'd had during his childhood in Harrow and unlike what he'd known for most of his adult life in the Navy, seemed a necessary priority. Having worked his way up to Master and a cabin, however tiny, of his own, James couldn't abide the idea of spending the rest of his working life living and sleeping in communal quarters. Finally, James wanted work which came with some freedoms: if not as his own boss, then at least in a job that was fairly independent and didn't require him to be answerable to long lines of superiors. If James could allow himself one more wish, it would be for a job out of doors, where he could content himself under an open sky. James was pleased with himself for devising such an orderly plan. The detail would need to be filled in later, but he knew many men who had reached the end of their naval career without the first clue of how to construct a new life. Such men had been subjected to Naval discipline, but they had never thought about how to make it work to their own advantage. James' lessons in Naval order, method and tactics, on the other hand, had been well learned and he was determined to use them for his future benefit.

When his ship reached England again, James took his discharge and travelled up to London. An old Navy friend offered James lodgings near Billingsgate Market and for a short while he considered working in the fish warehouses, but the dank chill of the buildings and the thought of smelling the sea but not seeing it, were unappealing. Then, just two weeks after leaving the ship, a chance encounter in a public house saw James being offered the opportunity to work as a coachman for a wealthy family in North Kensington. James was initially unsure, but a job out of doors, with reasonably flexible hours and the pleasure of being able to drive around London, sealed the deal for him. He still felt his fourteen-year-old self's antipathy towards the 'Yes, Sir, No, Sir,' brigade, but he was confident of managing that, after so many years in the Navy.

On his third day in his new career, James had cause to carry some of Madam's purchases into the main house. That was the first time that he saw his angel and he knew immediately that he was in love. The slight parlour maid with the beautiful, peachy complexion was called Jane and they discreetly courted for many months, as a relationship between servants would have not gone down favourably with the Mistress. On their days off, they would sit in Kensington Gardens and James would enchant Jane with tales of the high seas, of Port Royal and of Victor, the king of the former slaves. It wasn't one-sided. Jane had been brought up in Salthouse in Norfolk and narrated numerous entertaining stories of her fishing trips with her grandly-named father, Christmas Rudd. Their greatest joy was to take a small boat out on the lake and relive old memories. James Neary and Jane Rudd made a handsome couple and it was no surprise to their friends when, in the spring of 1872, they wed.

Fearing that one or both of them would be sacked, James and Jane decided, however, to keep their union secret from their employers. They didn't even dare tell their fellow servants in case their secret leaked out, but after a few months of marriage, their deception could no longer be sustained. Jane was expecting their first child and there was nothing to do but inform their employers of their marriage before the pregnancy became obvious. Enderby, the butler, told them that there had been quite a ding-dong upstairs. The Mistress was determined on instant dismissal for the pair of them, but the Master wouldn't hear of it. Neary had become a valued, loyal coachman and the Master saw no reason why he should have to leave. Unusually, in matters of the household, the Master had the last word and with the infant due at any time, he set the Nearys up in a flat above the stables, in Thorpe Mews.

It was in the Thorpe Mews flat that James Neary sat over a bowl of mutton stew, on the occasion of his fortieth birthday. It had been a rosy day. His brother, Henry, was enjoying a brief visit from Birmingham and together, they had taken little Emma Neary for a stroll along the Embankment. That evening, the Master, now widowed, had bought two tickets to the music hall for James and Jane. He had even offered the services of his old nanny, to tend to baby Emma during their absence.

James Neary felt a warmth in his belly that was nothing to do with the steaming stew. He couldn't wish for a more adorable, modern wife. His cheeky, adventurous daughter would keep his heart open for the rest of his life. He had work where he was trusted and a home where he was comfortable. The Navy had taught him discipline and he had developed a self-discipline that would stand him in good stead in his new role as provider for and protector of his family.

Yet just that afternoon, when Henry had taken Emma off to buy her a cornet, James had looked out across the water and felt memories stirring. A memory of the sea. A memory of the last time he stroked Genevieve's voluptuous contours. A memory of the last time he laid some flowers on Victor's grave. A memory of the church choir and one last song under the Jamaica stars. James smiled. What a wonderful collection of memories to carry with him through this new chapter in his life.

It would be quite an adventure to find out, now that he was married and living as a landlubber, whether he could he be the same man, with the same values, as the man with rank and respect who had fought so many bloody naval battles. Would he be able to find something to stir his soul to the same depth that he had felt when he faced up to those awe-inspiring Atlantic waves?

He had another question that was greater than all his other concerns combined. In his shore-dweller's middle-age, would he start settling for things, in the same way that his father and three brothers had always lived their lives in a rut? James chuckled. He used to rag Victor for his philosophical contemplations, but he had caught some of his old chum's ways. As Victor had often remarked, there's nothing like an expanse of water to encourage a man to question the meaning of his existence. That's what an afternoon on the Embankment does for you.

On the evening of his 40th birthday, James Neary made a vow. He would never again allow himself to be wrong-footed by philosophical gloominess. If life in the Navy had taught him anything, it was that it was a foolish occupation to keep looking backwards. It was not how he had lived his first forty years and he was not about to start now. He was blessed that he had a future.

22. Afternoon Tea In Bayswater

1913

There is something very appealing about a doily, a freshly ironed, crisp white doily with scalloped edging. It says something about the establishment. It says that this lodging house is a cut above some of the houses in this part of London, it is not one of the disreputable ones.

Mary Culley stood in her kitchen and arranged the thinly-sliced portions of sponge cake on to her best china display plate. The doily turned a respectable afternoon tea selection into something that could be admired. Home-made sponge cake, of course and some fine paste sandwiches with beautiful tomatoes from the Cheshers' allotment to top off the appetising display. It was a pity that only three of the residents were at home to sample the four o'clock feast, but there would be ample to go round.

Mary carried the tray into the front sitting room and set it down in pride of place on the sideboard. Her moment of silent satisfaction in her achievement was punctured by a loud snore coming from one of the window armchairs. Mrs. Atkinson was in deep slumber, probably on account of her consuming at least three sherries since midday. Never mind, she could smell a teapot from several floors away, so Mary was reassured that she would awaken shortly. Mary's other lady of private means, Mrs. Bennett, was away tending to an elderly aunt in Herne Bay and wasn't expected to return to London until the weekend. The two students, Mr. Singh and Mr. Prakash, were at their law chambers in Holborn, where they kept very long hours. The Chesher brothers were at work and they often chose to stop off for a wee dram before their return to the lodging house. So it was only going to be Mary, Mrs. Atkinson and Miss Nath Bose for afternoon tea.

Mary looked forward to four o'clock each day. After serving breakfast to her lodgers, her morning and the early part of the afternoon were occupied with cleaning. All her life, Mary had been a stickler for cleanliness and she wouldn't allow herself a sit-down until all the main rooms were given a good seeing-to. It wasn't her duty as the landlady to clean the residents' bedrooms, but Mary had a private arrangement with the two widows to dust and polish twice a week and today had been one of those days. In her dealings with Mrs. Atkinson, Mary often had cause to bite her tongue. Mrs. Atkinson, like Mary, had been widowed at a young age, but there the similarity between the two women ended. Mary was a worker who took her duties as a home-maker seriously. Her upbringing in Devon had been scarred by poverty, but she had always vowed never to forget the values of her parents and how they had worked their way out of the workhouse through good, honest toil. Then when she married William and became an army wife, she fostered a strong sense of duty which was only bolstered by the arrival of their two children. It was that sense of duty that drove Mary to provide the best possible conditions for her lodgers. She was in their service, but she wasn't a servant. Mrs. Atkinson's life had been considerably easier. She had never wanted for anything. Her family owned a large estate in Cambridgeshire, so she had been accustomed to being surrounded by an army of servants. Mary knew that old habits are difficult to break, but she couldn't help but feel resentful when Mrs. Atkinson went round after Mary's cleaning, running her index finger over the skirting boards. Mary remembered William's advice when he spoke about his sergeant-major: "Smile sweetly, dear, and then have a silent cuss when they are out of earshot."

The sitting room door creaked open and Miss Nath Bose entered the room. It is odd how you find companionship, thought Mary. Back in the days of Thorpe Mews, Mary would never have considered a friendship with a young slip of a thing from Africa, but over the past few weeks, Mary had found herself confiding some of her innermost thoughts to this stranger from another continent. In return, Miss Nath Bose had entertained Mary with tales that were so far out of Mary's own experience of the world, they could have been fairy stories. It struck Mary as charmingly ironic that Miss Nath Bose had experienced wealth not too dissimilar to Mrs. Atkinson's. Her father was a tribal leader and her mother was something important in their local church. Paying for their daughter to travel to England and live there for the three years of her study had caused the family no financial consternation.

The silence of the scene was interrupted by Mrs. Atkinson breaking wind very violently. She woke herself up with her eruption. As Mary predicted, the tea tray immediately caught the widow's eye and she heaved herself out of her armchair, with remarkable alacrity for one so slothful. Taking a small side plate, Mrs. Atkinson piled it high with paste sandwiches and three slices of cake. As she was about to retake her seat, she spotted Miss Nath Bose stoking the fire and tutted loudly. She hastily stuffed all the contents of her plate into the pocket of her dress and exited the room without a word of leave taking.

Mary tried to break the embarrassed quiet:

"Shall I be Mother, Miss Nath Bose?"

"That's very kind, Mrs.Culley. Just one small sandwich and half a slice of cake, please."

"Half a slice! You need filling up. Whoever heard of half a slice of my delicious cakes? My William could have eaten four whole slices without stopping for breath."

"Between you and me, Mrs.Culley, I have an admirer in the Faculty of Law. I need to keep my figure if he's not going to go off with some other pretty undergraduate."

"If he can't see what a diamond he's got in you, then he doesn't deserve you. Now, tuck into this whole slice. I'm not taking no for an answer."

The two women giggled like a pair of schoolgirls, despite the thirty year age difference between them, before sitting down to eat their afternoon tea in silence. As well as her strong sense of duty, manners were very important to Mary and she insisted that all meals must be taken without speaking. As Mary moved position in the chair that Mrs. Atkinson had recently vacated, she let out a small yelp of pain.

"What is it, Mrs.Culley?"

Mary rummaged under the cushion and pulled out a bottle of sherry. It had been prodding her in the bottom while she ate.

"Look at it! It's half full. I wouldn't put it past her to have cleaned off half a bottle since noon. I've seen it so many times in my life - bored women turning to the bottle in the hope of some temporary companionship."

Miss Nath Bose got up and started to clear away the tea things. Mary let her get on with it. When her daughter Annie had lived at home, Mary had insisted that Annie remove all the crockery after meals had been taken. Annie and Miss Nath Bose were a similar age. Mary gestured that she would hold on to her teacup, as they might have a reading of the tealeaves later.

Five minutes later, Miss Nath Bose returned to the sitting room, having washed and dried all the cups and plates. She was comfortable playing out this charade each day. She knew that the minute she left for the kitchen, Mrs. Culley would have filled up her cup to the brim with some of Mrs. Atkinson's sherry. She also knew that in about half an hour, she would have to listen to Mrs. Culley make her daily excuse that the leaves weren't quite settled enough for a proper reading. Today held a slight difference from the normal pantomime. As expected, Mrs. Culley was clutching her tea cup in such a way that the contents couldn't be seen, but she had also poured herself a second cup, which was resting on the nest of tables that Mary had pulled out for the occasion.

What followed was a familiar script. Mary encouraged Miss Nath Bose to tell her tales from her homeland. She was genuinely interested and asked a lot of relevant questions, but her concentration was poor, especially as her cup of sherry emptied; and after a few minutes, Mary would change the subject to her own life. Miss Nath Bose didn't mind. Some of her peers at University College were living in much more unsavoury accommodation, where they needed their wits about them at all hours of the day and night. Half an hour of a familiar story of woe was a small price to pay for safety and decent food. Miss Nath Bose was not one to mock another person's unhappiness, but she could have recited the daily script backwards.

The terrible fate of Mary's father in the asylum. Her husband's demise in the Boer war. Her son's foolish ambition to follow in his father's footsteps and Mary's daily fear of the fateful telegram. Her daughter's unsuitable marriage to the coachman's son and the shame of him being sacked from his job on the railway.

Fuelled by the second cup of sherry, Mary reached her daily crescendo:

"They've all deserted me. What price loyalty? That's the younger generation for you, present company excepted, Miss Nath Bose. Now I'm just a lonely old widow woman, waiting for the day when I'll be carried out of here in my coffin. I doubt they'll even turn up for my funeral. Can you imagine that, dear? Their sense of duty won't even stretch to their own mother's funeral."

Miss Nath Bose knew that this was poppycock. She had met Mary's daughter several times and although Annie could get exasperated at her mother's self-pity, she retained a loyalty and affection that was admirable. The son had been home on leave back in March and he had attended to his mother's every whim. He had even arranged a trip to the seaside for the whole lodging house and Annie came too, with her two little children. If Mary had been her own mother(and there were uncanny similarities) Miss Nath Bose might have been tempted to spell out some home truths. "I'm just a hopeless failure. I've failed as a wife. I've failed as a mother. I've been reduced to running a lodging house for all and sundry. My life is one long failure. Oh, my time is nigh....."

Miss Nath Bose strode over to the armchair that was accommodating her landlady. She snatched the cup from

Mary's hand and rummaged down the side of the cushion until she found the bottle. Before Mary could offer a word of admonition, Miss Nath Bose had placed both items on the sideboard.

"Now listen to me, Mother Culley. You are not a failure, quite the contrary. I know many women back home who have lost their husbands and their lives have finished. Some of them woe themselves to death, but not you, Mrs. Culley. You are sprung from stout stock. You found yourself on your own, stood yourself up, dusted yourself down and came and turned this place into a haven for the likes of me and all the other people on their own in London."

Mary was desperate to get a word in edgeways, but something in Miss Nath Bose's words and tone was penetrating all her usual defences.

"I won't hear more of this failure nonsense. You are a successful lady, Mrs.Culley and that should be celebrated, not mourned."

"Celebrated?"

"Celebrated. I will join you and we will praise God for his mercy and ask him to keep you in the successful manner to which you have become accustomed."

Miss Nath Bose returned to the sideboard and poured two more cups of sherry. Mary stood up in anticipation of the toast.

"To success and friendship."

The door creaked open and Mrs. Atkinson returned.

"Here, that's my sherry. You've polished off the whole bottle!"

The other two ladies barely heard her. They had success and friendship to celebrate.

23. Eight Photos

2020

Lockdown. Covid-19 Britain.

I had lots of time on my hands. In my bedroom at Steven's house, there is a large, walk-in cupboard. It's a strange shape, because it fits under the stairs to the flat above. Although we've only been there since 2016, the cupboard has become the repository for everything that doesn't fit anywhere else. It's a mess, quite frankly. So, I decided to use a locked-down weekend to sort it out.

Having taken everything out and filled two rubbish sacks, it was time to put everything back. We keep spare CD and DVD players for Steven, so they were the first items to go back. I tried to push them into the corner, but something was blocking their passage. I got down on all fours and crawled into the cupboard. Scrunched up in the corner was a solitary boot. Goodness knows where the other half of the pair had gone. It was once a favourite boot, now about 25 years old. Cool at the time, but too scuffed since to be seen in high society. It was time to say farewell to my boot.

As I went to throw the boot into the bin, I noticed something sticking out of the top. For a minute I went back to 1984. I collect overheard conversations. I've compiled a book of them. One of my favourites goes back to my time working at Ealing council and happened at the clocking-in machine. It was snowing. I was clocking back in from my lunch break

237

and two women were clocking out for theirs. They were deep in conversation:

"And I felt the most peculiar sensation and it was coming from the inside of my boot."

"Didn't you take it off and have a look?"

"I did. And it was green."

And off they went.

I never found out what was the green thing inside her wellington. The content of my boot was much more familiar. A lump rose in my throat as soon as I saw what it was. Back in 1991, my sister and I were clearing out my Dad's belongings after he died and found the tiniest photo album you've ever seen. It was no bigger than a cigarette packet. It was brown and had just three plastic compartments, containing six pictures. Almost 30 years later, it had fallen off the shelf into my boot and I had nearly thrown it away.

When I got home later that day, I took all the photos out for closer examination. It was a surgical procedure. They had been in the small wallet for at least 50 years and were very delicate. I was petrified of accidentally tearing them. As they came out, I discovered that there were a couple of additional photos that Dad had squeezed between the ones that were visible.

There were eight photos. What were they saying?

One was of him and Mum and two of their friends. Mum and Dad are in their early twenties. The other man is preposterously tall. He's not standing on anything raised, but he towers over 5'8" Dad. They had a friend called Bunny Austin, who wasn't the same Bunny Austin who played at Wimbledon. Is this giant of a man Bunny Austin? Sadly, there is nobody around who will remember the name of Mrs Austin. The photo is in black and white, obviously. Dad has a very fetching centre parting. I don't have any memories of him with a centre parting.

There was another photo of a very young Dad with a buttonhole. It's not his wedding. I know my parents' wedding photos like the back of my hand. Perhaps it's his brother Stan's wedding day? They were close. The photo has been cut badly, so that Dad is the only person in the picture. Is this an unusual sign of vanity on Dad's part, that he's cut the other people in the photo out? He might still be a teenager.

There was an intriguing photo that's been cut in half. It's one of those Woolworth photo-booth photos. It looks like there is a woman in the missing part of the snap: a glimpse of a cheek, a few shreds of her hair. There's not much to go on, but it doesn't look like Mum. Is it an old flame of Dad's, pre-Mum? An unrequited love? Dad is in a cardigan and tie. There's the subtle hint of a kiss-curl, but it's not in the centre of his head. Whoever the woman is, you can see why she would have been attracted to him.

There was a photo of me and him. I'm about two. It's a very windy day. In the wind, his hair looks longer than at any time that I can remember. He's pushing me in my buggy, along what looks like a causeway. There's a boat in the distance. I'm in tartan shorts.

There was an identity card for Mum. It's from the early days of their marriage, when they were still living with Mum's mother. The box labelled, 'In the event of an emergency, contact...' is empty. The back of the card has several boxes that act as reminders to get things done. 'Driving Licence expires', 'Fire insurance due', 'Radio licence due'. My parents weren't organised about getting things done. They needed reminders when things were due. There was a mix-up with my school enrolment and I didn't start Infant school until January. Someone missed registering me for the September start. There was no box on the identity card that said, 'Remember to book your son into school.'

There were three photos taken on a family trip to the seaside. It must have been a special occasion, because it looks like both sides of the family were on the excursion. I'm there in my pushchair, stationed in front of Dad's mum, Annie Culley. I'm drinking from a bottle of milk and have a bucket and spade on my lap. To the right is clearly Uncle Charlie and next to him, hidden behind an open newspaper, I'm pretty sure is Uncle Albert Farwell. Both men are from the Worley side of the family. How did the two families come together for the day? Did it involve charabancs? It stretches my comprehension to its limits, as I cannot imagine two families coming together in such numbers in modern times.

The final photo was of soldiers. It's a very long shot, so it's impossible to make out any faces. I think it's World War Two. It might be in India. They've set up a camp. Everyone looks deadly serious. It's not a staged, posed photograph. The men are either lolling about or unpacking their kit bags into their tents. I can't find any family resemblances, but I suspect that it must be Dad's brother, Reg. Dad kept Reg's medals, but never spoke about him. Reg was sixteen years older than Dad. With an age gap like that, I wonder whether they were close.

That's it. Since my discovery, I've been left with two questions. Why were those eight photos so important to Dad that he kept them so close to him in his bedside drawer? And what is their message to me? What are they saying about Lines?

The first question, I can have a stab at. That day back in 1991, I found something else in Dad's bedside drawer. It was one of my 'miscellaneous' It books. It was from 1973/74 and had a collection of song lyrics I had written. As you know, I was heavily into The Sweet and T Rex at the time and the songs had titles like: 'The Cosmic Garden of Joy' and 'Midnight Rave Up At The Ritz'. Dad kept that book for nearly 20 years, but never once said to me that he was proud of my lyrical flair. He was an actions man, not a words man. I suspect that the keeping of these photos come from a similar place within him. Everyone who knew Dad spoke of how he kept his own counsel. He was a man of few words. The family story goes that my Mum was told about a potential suitor for her, who drank in The Halfway House: "He doesn't talk much, but he's got an infectious laugh."

I'm pretty sure that if he were still around today and I asked him about the eight photos, he would have very little to say on the subject. At one of the lowest times in my life, our baby had just died and I turned up at Dad's for some familiar company. He greeted me at the door and put his arm around my shoulder. No words were spoken. Then he disappeared into the kitchen and came back with a cold steak and kidney pie for me. That's how he did things. It was exactly what I needed.

What is the message for Lines? We know everything about our lines. We know nothing about our lines. My lines are different from his. The photos bring together all the people and themes I've written about in this book. They are the past, the present and the future. The people and the values they represent have shaped me and are what provide with my meaning to this day.

Or they might just be one of the book's final conundrums. The photos throw up far more questions than they do answers, so perhaps they are simply confirmation that I know sod all. I am pretty sure that in several years time, someone will be clearing out my boots and come across the things that have been important in my life. They may well be touched by their discovery, but as sure as eggs are eggs, they will question why those items carried such value for me.

24. The Wedding.

2019.

It arrived last week. It was in amongst the leaflets touting half price kebabs and the letter from the council, advising me that it's time to review Steven's care package. Deep joy. The offer of a greasy slice of unidentifiable-origin meat and the annual threat that our life could be turned upside down.

Still, as the wise woman said, "In every bucket of cold sick, an oyster pearl may be found." The third piece of correspondence was a wedding invitation. The card invited me and a guest of my choosing to a wedding on 14th March at St John's Church, in Southall. As the nuptials were being held in our home town, I decided to ask my sister if she wanted to be the guest of my choosing. The only slight problem was that there was a nasty grease stain on the card, so it was impossible to make out the names of the bride and groom. Perhaps they were eating a kebab whilst writing it.

Thirty minutes later, Jayne phoned. She had received exactly the same invitation. She had been racking her brain for ages, as her invitation carried a matching kebab stain. We didn't know anyone who lives in Southall anymore. If it were one of our relatives, then surely we would have heard about it. Yet Jayne's curiosity, like mine, had been aroused and we made a pact to attend. She suggested that she bring her grandson

Henry and I decided to take Steven. I thought that I had better bring two of the support workers, incognito. Jayne was a little bemused by my suggestion that perhaps we should go in period costume. Nothing definite, but I had a tiny inkling of what might be happening.

By the time we were just three days from the wedding, I was pretty sure that I knew what was going on, but although I might consider myself an old hand at this time travel business, I didn't want to get blasé. Did I need to tip Jayne off? After all, she hadn't been to Shoalstone Pool, or Brentford Docks, or listened to 'Mamma Mia' with a very special guest. I had been a bit circumspect about those encounters, because I value my liberty. On the other hand, I didn't want Jayne to have an attack of the vapours in the middle of King Street.

The fourteenth of March arrived and we all piled into the camper van. I was nervous that we had gone a bit overboard, because Steven, Francis, Michael and I were kitted out and resembled a multi-racial Bill Haley and his Comets. Jayne had got her decades a bit mixed up, so she and Henry looked like Vera Lynn and a little waif about to be evacuated to the countryside. Because Steven had come unstuck trying to devise a wedding compilation tape and because Henry is only six, we took along a 100-Track CD of 'Children's Timeless Favourites'. We were quite the band of travelling minstrels, singing along to 'The Laughing Policeman'.

I hadn't told Jayne about my suspicions and I was feeling dead guilty. I would have been very pissed off, if the boot had been on the other foot. And what about Henry? How do you begin to explain what's about to happen to a six-year-old? I should have realised that I didn't need to worry. As we drove into Western Road, Steven piped up:

"Auntie Jayne! We're going to a wedding! Like Alan and Jean in Fawlty Towers."

"I know, sweetheart."

"Going to a wedding. Steven Neary's going to see Granddad John and Nanny Beryl get married."

With the exasperation that only someone of six can carry off, Henry said, "We know that, Steven!"

We had arrived, and it was all a little overwhelming. The Comets took Steven and Henry to find a seat at the back of the church. Steven was beside himself, because he reckoned that he was about to see a recreation of the church scene from 'Muriel's Wedding' and he expected everyone to enter the church to the strains of 'I Do, I Do, I Do'. Jayne led me to a discreet spot under a tree. We were attracting quite a bit of attention from the locals. My outfit was a couple of years ahead of its time and Jayne's ensemble hadn't been seen around these parts since VE Day.

Jayne whispered, "They're all here." She was right.

Our cousins Jean and Hazel were the bridesmaids, Jean looking a picture of elegance, although to me, she was almost unrecognisable as the Jean that I grew up with during her Dusty Springfield-inspired days. Hazel was so young, but then she was a few years away from successfully auditioning for The Tiller Girls and being rewarded with a summer season with Billy Dainty. On the Neary side of the family, Uncle Stan was Dad's best man. We never met him in the flesh, because he emigrated to Australia in 1954. He looked like he had got everything under control. He was especially keeping an eye out for Uncle Frank, who appeared happy and was trying to thread a piece of cable through his buttonhole.

What happened next was a piece of pure theatre. From the left of the church, all of Dad's sisters appeared, arms linked. Simultaneously, from the opposite side, the Worley women made their grand entrance. All it needed was for Hazel to join them in the middle, put on a top hat, and lead them in a can-can. Auntie Phil would have been her perfect, literal sidekick for it. When I knew her, Phil had developed rheumatism and was never seen out of trousers, but she always used to bring up that she'd had lovely legs in her salad days. She wasn't wrong. I had never seen a shapelier pair of pins.

The main car arrived and everybody started to scuttle off into the church. Jayne and I stood rooted to the spot. As I had told the Comets to get a back row seat, we could sneak in after everyone was seated. Besides, I wasn't entirely sure that we were visible to the congregation's naked eye.

Uncle Charlie got out of the car first. Jayne wiped away a small tear, because jointly with his brother Uncle Albert, Charlie was always her favourite. "Whacker Worley", they called him, the boy who, when he was twelve, ran away from home to join the circus, where he performed a strongman act. The man who used to leave me awestruck when he showed off his party trick, which entailed eating a whole Granny Smith apple in one bite. The man who died, that Christmas Eve when the rest of us were holidaying in Bournemouth. Uncle Charlie had taken on the rôle of giving his sister away, as their father had passed on three years earlier.

Finally, Mum appeared from the car. I had looked through her wedding album hundreds of times. In fact it's open on my desk now, as I write this chapter, but in none of the photos does she look as radiant as she did in the flesh. By a strange quirk of forty-year fate, she looked a tiny bit like Muriel Heslop. I was half-tempted to dash in and to warn Steven that although there was a certain receding-hairline similarity, Uncle Whacker wasn't Bill Heslop, so he wouldn't be saying, "She's all yours, mate," as he handed the bride over to Granddad John.

We slipped unnoticed into the church and it was a relief to see that Steven was lapping everything up. Most of the congregation he knew only from the collage of the family tree

248

that I have pinned up on the living room wall, although he had met some of the guests in the mid nineties, before the sudden onslaught of deaths in the latter part of the decade drastically pruned the living branches. He still recognised everybody. He likes to quote Mrs Boynton in 'Appointment With Death'- "Once seen, I never forget a face"– and it is absolutely true. He was calling out across the pews:

"Auntie Rose! It's Steven Neary here! I'm a man now."

Steven is very interested in his history and the family stories. There is a word, 'griot', for West African storytellers who act as their villages' oral historians. You may recall the scene at the end of the final episode of Roots, where Alex Haley travelled to Ghana and eventually found the griot. After listening for hours, Haley started to feel impatient, but then the griot mentioned Kunta Kinte and Haley finally discovered the origins of his African ancestor, two hundred years after Kinte was kidnapped and enslaved. Being unable to read or write, Steven is the griot of the Neary/Worley/Culley/Fleetwood history. After I have told him a story from the past, I will hear Steven in bed, later that night, logging all the necessary information. "Granddad John's daddy was a man called Henry Neary...."

"Uncle Bob! It's Steven Neary here. We've got your van."

The ceremony passed smoothly. We nipped out before the bride and groom departed the church. We had already decided not to hang about for the photos. I knew that Steven had been chatting away to everyone and they had been talking to him, but I was not sure that Jayne and I had been noticed. That was okay. It wouldn't have felt right to be in the photos anyway. The Comets, Steven and Henry had already got into the van and Henry was trying to pick up the lyrics to 'Right Said Fred'. Steven was explaining to him that Bernard Cribbins is also Mr Hutchinson from Fawlty Towers, who got a bit of cheese stuck in his throat. Jayne and I were just about to get in, when we heard a voice.

"Chicks?"

It was Dad. He leaned forwards to give us both a hug and accidentally dropped his buttonhole in a puddle. Uncle Frank darted forward, picked up the carnation, and tried to thread it back through Dad's jacket with the piece of cable. The photographer called Dad away because it was time for the photo with the parents. As we drove off, he knocked on the window and mouthed, "Thanks."

We drove to The Halfway House, where the reception was being held. As we pulled into the car park that the pub shared with Southall FC's Western Road ground, I suddenly remembered the date. We were in 1953. I have a press cutting at home from the 1953 season that described 'the tenacious Neary, tearing down the wing.' Dad probably would have been on the teamsheet today, but had to channel his tenacity into getting married instead.

I could see that the floodlights at the football club were switched on. I could hear the orchestra of wooden rattles, and the familiar chant of "Up the 'hall." I saw Jim Humble, emptying his lawn mower into one of the industrial bins. I thought back to 1995 and the summer that we adopted Steven. I had taken him to the Halfway House, even though I had known that Southall's ground had been bulldozed a couple of years before. I had still wanted to show Steven any remnants that there might have been of my spiritual home. There had been nothing to see except the newly-built blocks of flats.

Jayne saw me looking across at the stands and read my mind.

"What do you want to do? Do you want to go in?"

"Do you mind?"

"Of course not. Who cares if we are ridiculously overdressed for a football match, and the guys will get their nuts frozen off? Let's go in and cheer on the 1953 version of Alan Devonshire."

As we joined the queue at the turnstile, the wedding cars started to arrive. The thought struck me that, apart from our grandparents, Jayne and I were probably the oldest people at the wedding. Not yet born, but the most senior of the guests. How was that for a lovely headmelt?

Jayne came over and put her arm around my shoulder.

"You okay?"

"Yeah. I'm fine thanks. It's just that it's not our day, today. This is where we belong, but not yet. This is their time."

Two hours later, we emerged, freezing, from the match. We had been doing the next best thing to taking Bovril intravenously, but our shivers were all of a quiver. Three-nil to the 'hall. As we climbed into the van for our last look at Southall, until 1959 and 1966 respectively, the door of the Halfway House was flung open, and Auntie Hilda led a conga to the top of Scotts Road and back. I could hear familiar laughter and Auntie Phil's voice purring: "What do you reckon then? Don't you think I've got a lovely pair of legs?"

Henry, who had been asleep for the past fifteen minutes, sat bolt upright and started singing:

"So Charlie and me
Had another cup of tea
And then we
Went home."

25. The Publican

1881

It was a cheery Saturday afternoon in Southall in 1881. To say that there was a sense of expectation in the air would be putting it mildly. Four young people were preparing excitedly for their big night. Isabella Worley was giving the privy door one last coat of paint. She had dismissed the others' concerns that the paint might not be dry in time. She pointed at the sun, flaming yellow overhead, and told them to sling their hooks. Besides, Isabella enjoyed painting. She appreciated the satisfaction of transforming something old into something that the customers would admire. The decorating also distracted Isabella from her worries about the evening ahead. At nineteen, she was old enough to be keenly aware of her responsibilities, but young enough to not be constrained by the burden of unrealistic expectations. Isabella recalled the day that she broke the news to her father that she and Charlie would be taking on the running of a public house. She still felt deeply hurt that her father refused to share her enthusiasm. In fact, he had actively discouraged her from going ahead with their project. This was so unlike him. To have her dreams dismissed as 'a fool's mission' upset her greatly. She knew only too well that her father viewed Charlie as 'a dreamer' with 'every new idea, as feckless as the one that came before it'. What her father was blind to, though, was

Charlie's steely determination to get ahead in life. Sometimes, it quite shook Isabella that Charlie saw hurdles only as an obstacle to be trampled down. Isabella could never expect her father to see what she saw in Charlie and she could never admit to her father that what drew them together was the thrill of living life on the edge of lawlessness. Although Charlie was not traditionally handsome, his swagger had attracted Isabella from the first time she had set eyes on him, and she had soon discovered that he could charm the birds out of the trees and herself out of her strait-laced habits. Having been brought up under a weight of Christian piety, Isabella was guiltily excited to discover that she revelled in the thrill of sneaking through the back of the Cranford estate with Charlie on rabbit-poaching expeditions. Danger was always present, but the allure of Charlie's boldness and his eye for some easy money, outweighed the threat. She also recognised Charlie's loyalty. When his mother lost her mind and was admitted into the lunatic asylum, Isabella saw Charlie throw a protective wing over his younger siblings. So it was that Sarah and John were here, living with them over the pub and sharing in their exciting adventure. Isabella picked up her pot of sky-blue paint and whistled a merry tune as she completed her work.

For the last five minutes, Charles had been observing Isabella from his position in the ale yard. What a proper stunner his wife was. Charles knew that all his chums back in Studds Lane had the hots for his little beauty and it pleased him no end that he had managed to catch such a filly from under their noses. One of his mates had once described Isabella as 'a beautiful saucepot' and Charles took great pride in the knowledge that later that day, his beautiful saucepot would be on display for the whole of Southall to see. A man could be anyone, go anywhere with such a beauty on his arm. Those nights creeping through the Cranford undergrowth, checking rabbit snares had showed Charlie that he'd picked a woman who was prepared to take life by the scruff of the neck and adept at doing so. Even after their son had died at just four weeks old earlier that year, Isabella had quickly regained her figure and her enthusiasm for her man and for life itself. When he compared his wife to his mad old mother, he recognised that he had landed sunny side up in bagging such an effervescent creature. When the subject of running a pub had first come up, just two weeks after the little one died, Charles knew that he could count on Isabella to stand by him and help his dream come true. Spurred on by his mixture of pride and love, Charles picked Isabella up by the waist and swung her around the yard.

"Put me down, you daft younker. I've got me paint going everywhere."

This only made Charlie more cheerful and proud. He swaggered to the centre of the yard.

"Look at all of this, Bella. Our new start. Me and you."

"It will work, won't it, Charlie?"

"I dunno. We'll give blood, sweat and tears to make it work and if it doesn't, we would have had bloody good fun, giving it a go. What is life for if it's not for having a bit of fun."

Charles returned Isabella to the ground and they enjoyed a long, lingering kiss. Their moment of bliss was interrupted by thirteen-year-old Sarah, running excitedly into the yard.

"I've done it, Charlie. What do you think? Where shall I put it?"

Charles took the sheet of paper that Sarah offered to him and smiled. His sister had never been much of an artist and this effort was rudimentary at best, but she wanted to play her part in the big day. She had an unwavering belief in her brother. With pride, Charles read aloud the words on the child's poster:

"The Kings Head, Southall. Every Saturday night. Singing. Dancing. Storytelling. Hosted by your landlords - Mr. and Mrs. Charles Worley."

"It's perfect, Sis. And I want it displayed in pride of place, in the centre of the front window."

Satisfied, Sarah skipped off, delighted to display her artwork. Isabella followed her, as she only had a couple of hours to try and wash the paint out of her hair. Charles was left alone in the yard and he proudly perched himself on a barrel. He thought about his peers, giving their souls through their toil in the brick fields. At twenty, what future did they have to look forward to? Charles truly believed that he had the whole world in his twenty-year-old hands. He surveyed all around him. He swelled with pride at the sight of this grand establishment that in a few hours time would be packed with thirsty revellers. He looked across the yard to the ruddy-faced boatmen cruising past, each with an eye to his horse, lest the towlines become tangled. There were dozens of moored barges and very soon, those hard-working bargemen would be handing over their hard-earned cash and drinking the night away. Charles felt satisfied that his pub was in the perfect spot to draw in the trade even though Isabella's father, Mr Thomas Webb, had looked down his nose when he paid a flying visit yesterday. With a contemptuous glance at the bargemen, Mr Webb had snorted, "You will be the ruin of my daughter. I don't want her in the company of beasts like them." If any other man had been so rude, Charles would have showed him his knuckles. He wondered whether Mr Thomas Webb had made such a success of his life at such a young age. Charles had always lived off his wits and look at what he had achieved so far having adopted that approach to life. Neither Mr Webb, nor his own father for that matter, could hold a candle to Charlie when it came to, as the old poet had said, sucking the marrow out of life.

John hobbled into the yard. Charles chuckled as he watched his fifteen-year-old brother haphazardly trying to balance a full keg on his developing shoulders. John almost fell arse over tip as he attempted to prop open the cellar door.

"Oi, little 'un. Put your back into it."

"Go and fluff yourself, brother. You could always give me a hand."

"And then you'd learn nothing. Get on with it."

Charles took out his pipe. What a time to be alive! Everything was expanding: the public houses, the music halls, the football grounds, the municipal gardens. They called them 'Palaces of Pleasure', and here he was, Charles Worley, in his very own palace.

Charles thought about his own father, thirty years ago, standing in those vast, empty fields of Southall and vowing to build a better world. He thought about his wretched grandfather, wrecked by poverty and destined to die in the workhouse. Was he looking down from heaven at his grandson's success? Did his father know, in the old days, that places like the Kings Head would be the symbols of the better world that he was creating? He hoped that his father would be here tonight, to bear witness.

10 o'clock.

The evening was shaping up nicely. The local Southallians might not have approved of the hordes of rowdy men, but their inebriation was music to the ears of Charles. Old Mrs Aspen had done a sterling job playing all the old tunes on the piano and had kept the customers' spirits high for over two hours. A fight had broken out between four young boatmen, but despite his build being slight, Charles' demeanour was authoritative and the aggression was quickly extinguished. John spotted a woman who was trying to purchase some gin with counterfeit coins and with some firm words and a boot up her backside, dealt with the matter swiftly. Isabella had been all for calling the rozzers, but there had been no need. Charles had never been prouder of his little brother.

One mistake that Charles had made was to underestimate the number of bar staff needed. He had anticipated that he and Isabella would work the bar between them, whilst John and Sarah tended to all the backroom jobs, but they needed more people out front. Singing and dancing can quickly build up a thirst and within the first hour, Charles had to call upon the assistance of two chums and his father, who had called by 'to see how the land lay'. Serving drunken boatmen was not William's idea of spending a productive Saturday night, but he rolled up his sleeves and took on the role of collecting the empty tankards. He would save his ragging of Charlie until the doors were closed.

The storytelling was well under way. Mrs Stokey recited a long, gruesome piece of poetry about the dentist, Mr Green, who had removed all of her mother's teeth. A pretty young Miss told a long story about the correct combination of blooms to make up a lady's wedding bouquet. She was noisily heckled by some of the boatmen and fled the stage in tears. One of the boat skippers was next up and told the ribald tale of his saucy evening spent with an Oxford farm girl. The evening was in danger of falling flat when Mr Joyce, the tobacconist, delivered a monologue about the lush terrain of the Yorkshire Moors. A young hoodlum, standing next to the raised platform, started banging the table with cries of, "Skittle ye off, old-timer!"

For the first time that evening, Charles felt apprehensive as he mounted the platform, whilst encouraging the audience to applaud Mr Joyce for the "enlightening tales of his travels." An awkward silence fell over the pub. Charles coughed nervously as one or two people hissed,

"Get on with it, man!"

Charles appealed for further storytellers, but none were forthcoming. Anxious that unrest might break out, Charles cleared his throat for one last time:

"Thank you. I just want to tell you a story about a very special lady.....
There was a fine girl, name of Bella
Who married a disreputable fella   ("Hoorah!")
At the altar they stood
Before the great and the good
Praising heaven and not the devil's cellar."   ("Boo. Not the devil's cellar!")

Charles was struggling. He had turned as red as a beetroot. He had developed an unaccustomed stammer. Isabella, noticing his panic, jumped onto the platform:

"Their child, he had succumbed at 4 weeks

His constitution was sadly too meek.

His parents' hearts felt such love

As they prayed to their ghosts up above

And they vowed that the good times, they would immediately seek."

The customers clapped and cheered. William Worley junior stood up and shook his son's hand. Isabella performed a saucy curtsey to the audience, leaving the hecklers red-faced. With renewed confidence, Charles announced to the drunken throng:

"That's my missus, ladies and gentlemen. Drinks all round. Let's drink Southall dry."

It was 2 o'clock the following morning. The last drinker had left at ten minutes past midnight. Having run on adrenaline all day, Charles and Isabella were finding it difficult to wind down. Contentment was present, but sleep would be a long time coming. Eventually, Isabella spoke:

"You do realise that you've scuppered any profits we may have made with your boozy largesse tonight?"

"We'll think about profits when we open the doors again, tomorrow. Tonight was about good sport."

"We can't always be relying on tomorrow, Charlie."

"Hey. Don't I always make things right? Whenever, I've been in a hole, I can always magic up a spade to dig myself out. What's one night's takings when we're talking about the rest of our lives?"

"You've always had confidence in spades. I'll give you that much. That poem? Were you making it up as you went along?"

"Couldn't you tell? Give a man six brandies and he believes that he's Mr. Wordsworth."

Isabella and Charles fell into each other's arms, laughing their socks off.

Charles remembered a conversation with his grandfather just after Willam Snr. had been released from gaol. Addled by the drink and the early stages of a frightened madness, William Worley could still occasionally deliver some words of wisdom.

"If you can't see the good days whilst they are happening, your mind will be eaten away by the bad ones."

As Isabella drifted off to sleep, Charles repeated his grandfather's words to a passing swan and said a silent prayer for his mother.

26. Changing Direction.

2020.

A smaller grouping than the one that assembled at Florence Road in 1973 for Uncle Bob's big moment, has gathered in Steven's living room. There are Steven, Alan and me, plus William Culley, popping in after his experiences in the Boer War. Steven is in a tetchy mood. He fancies having a Beautiful South music session, but I've commandeered the television for my big moment. He is mildly amused by the two pigeons, bobbing their heads and cooing in a cage that is perched precariously on the window sill. He makes a joke to William about, "Two dead pigeons in the water tank. Take them out." As William died in 1901, this Manuel joke flies straight over his head. Jayne and her partner, Wayne, arrive with Pringles. That lifts Steven's mood greatly. The end credits of 'Match of the Day' start to roll. Ever loyal, Alan tries to bring the room to order and focus on the telly.

"Ssh, everyone. It's starting."

I know what is coming and I am nervous. It's surprising how many cheese footballs you can absent-mindedly consume when you've got butterflies in your belly.

Dee dee da da da dum dum.
Dee dee da da dum dum dum."

Oh, that theme tune takes you back. William feeds a Wotsit to the pigeons. They aren't impressed. Steven takes his leave, muttering something about taking Paul Heaton to the bedroom.

"Good evening, and welcome to the Parkinson Show. My name is Michael Parkinson. My three guests tonight all have something in common. They have all had moments in their lives where they abruptly and unexpectedly changed direction. Later I will be talking to the tennis legend, Martina Navratilova and (insert) to the author of the runaway best-selling book, 'Lines' - Mark Neary. But my first guest tonight is an actor, quiz show host, raconteur, keen cricketer and all-round national treasure. Ladies and gentlemen, please welcome....Nicholas Parsons."

Nicholas gingerly descends the famous long staircase and he and Parky embrace warmly.

"Nicholas, you were a marine engineer after leaving school. Tell me how you made the switch to acting..."

The doorbell rings. Alan goes to answer it.

"Well, Michael, I always had ambition towards the stage, but never knew how to get started. As a child, I was terribly precocious. At school, they used to call me 'Shirley', after Shirley Temple...."
Alan returns.

"It's the delivery man. You had better come and see. I think he's got the wrong house. He says his name is Charlie"
I go out to the hall and there is a young chap standing in the porch, with a crate of beers balanced on his knee.

"Come on, old man. Give us a hand with this lot. I've got another two out here..."

Alan and I help our latest guest carry the drinks through to the kitchen. I haven't ordered a delivery. Perhaps it's a complimentary present from Parky. He's well known for being partial to the amber nectar, so this may be his way of saying, "Thanks." The delivery man whips six bottles out of the crate and bolts into the living room.

"Now then, when does this party get started? Here you go, soldier boy. Get this down your neck. Budge up, Jayne. Make some room for your great-grandfather."

Of course. Charlie is Charlie Worley, but the Charlie of his glory days in the Kings Head, twenty years old, as fit as a butcher's dog and as full as bonhemie and zest as a Jack Russell terrier. It wasn't the Charlie of a couple of years later: unwell, slightly punctured and back working in the brick fields like his father. He shoots a quick glance at me and for a brief moment, I think I detect something pleading in that glance. I smile at him as reassuringly as I can. Beer-bribe or not, I'm not going to shatter his front, least of all in the middle of a party. After all, I know as well than most, how important it can feel to keep up a front when you're feeling at your most fragile. He may have lost the pub, but the way that Charlie is flirting with my sister shows that he hasn't lost any of his Del-Boy.

Steven has returned to the room and is loving the new arrival.

"Hello, Charlie. Go up to the roof and take the two dead pigeons out of the water tank."

Charlie gives Steven a playful punch in the belly. Wayne and William are sharing stories of how your football career can be easily curtailed by a nasty injury. Wayne sustained a career-threatening injury back in the mid 1990s, but William is always going to trump anything that Wayne can come up with. Fair play to him, he holds back on his anecdote about Albert Jackson and his missing leg.

"Thank you, Nicholas. Now, what can I say about my next guest? Nine times Wimbledon champion, the winner of seventeen grand slam titles. Ladies and gentlemen...Martina Navratilova...."

"The thing is, Jayne, I wanted more from life than being a brick labourer. I'm not knocking my old man. It served him well and he had a swell time, doing what he loved. Christ, he built the town that you grew up in. But it wasn't for me...."

"So, Martina, how big a change was it when you moved from Czechoslovakia to America?"

"He could do things with a ball that would bring tears of admiration to your eyes..."

The doorbell rings again. I think that I have given up on Parky and my sudden change of direction into Saturday night light entertainment. Too much is going on, so I go and open the door. Standing there is a ridiculously handsome man in a bowler hat.

"Excuse me, Sir, for calling at this late hour. I just happened to be passing in my coach and I couldn't help noticing that wonderful camper van parked outside. Is it yours? Forgive my forwardness, but I was wondering if you were prepared to sell it. Oh my goodness. Where are my manners? I haven't introduced myself. Here is my card..."

He hands over a perfectly embossed cream card. Patrick Bateman would have to kill him out of envy. The card reads, 'Alfred Gwynne Vanderbilt'.

"Come in, Sir. We are just having a ....family get-together. Please come and join us."

I escort Alfred into the living room, where a game of musical chairs has taken place and everyone has changed seats. Wayne is chatting to the pigeons in much the same way as he would to his own birds. Steven is showing William his photo album. Charlie has assumed the role of barman. The second crate of ale is on the dining-room table. I introduce Mr. Vanderbilt to the company. Charlie plays the host and offers him a beer.

"You're a proper dandy, like I've never seen before. Terrible tragedy about you and the ship. You have my condolences."

"William. The man with the glasses on is a man called Gilbert Best. Gilbert Best was Steven Neary's teacher at Grangewood. Gilbert Best is wearing a red jumper and grey trousers. Julie Neary has got the camera....."

"Coooee, Esther. You're a beautiful, little bird, aren't you?"

"And my final guest tonight is an unusual man. He's the bestselling author and the ace face of the over-sixties Mod movement. Ladies and gentlemen. Mar...."

The doorbell rings. It's Des. He's collected cousins Jean and Hazel at the top of the road. Hazel is showing Jean that she can still kick her leg up as high as the washing line. Des has arrived for the night shift. He's due to take over from Alan, but I'm not sure that Alan wants to clock off yet. I try to fill Des in, but don't know where to start with the shift handover. It doesn't matter, so I offer Des a beer, instead. Des gets the set-up in seconds.

Back in the living room, William and Jayne are chatting about stable boys and farming. Charlie and Wayne are on to the third crate. Alan and Alfred Vanderbilt are discussing Nigerian politics. Hazel and Jean are doing a jive without a musical accompaniment. Watching their jive, I'm reminded that back in the early 1970s, people used to dance with their wrists much more than they do these days. Hazel is a prime example of the decline of wrist dancing, made even more noticeable in that she has long since ditched the charm bracelet that used to jangle from her wrist. The New Year's Eve parties were dangerous playgrounds. If you weren't careful during 'Love Grows Where My Rosemary Goes', Hazel could have your eye out with her lethal charms.

"Of course, my father was a farmer, as was his father before him. And, do you know, Jayne? I would have been perfectly happy to stay on the farm. But for men of my generation, the army gave us the opportunity to travel. To see the world...."

"Well, of course, Mr Alan, but we've got that wily old Presidential fox, Woodrow Wilson...."

"Wayne, old son. If you want to make yourself a bit of money and have a bit of a laugh in the process, get yourself a pub...."

"Mark, my final question. What do you think it is, within you, which opened the door to such a big change of direction at sixty?"

Jayne's daughter, Jodie, is standing in the doorway, carrying a fast-asleep Henry.

"Mum! Dad! What time do you call this? I thought something....."

Charlie grabs her by the hand and leads her in an extravagant waltz.

"You're a cute one, aren't you? Now tell me, Wayne. What is she to me? Great-granddaughter or great-great.....?"

Someone has opened the birdcage and Job the pigeon has just crapped over the telly. On screen, I've got bird poo running down my cheek.

Steven has returned, having found his Beautiful South playlist on Spotify. He is wearing Alfred Gwynne Vanderbilt's bowler hat.

"I want my sun drenched, windswept, Ingrid Bergman kiss.
Not in the next life.
I want it, in this."

I grab Steven's hand and we dance our little hearts out to one of Mr Heaton's greatest moments. Hazel is leading everyone else in a can-can.

The phone rings. Des does an 'excuse me' and takes over dancing with Steven, whilst I go to answer the phone.

"Hello. Yes, it's Mark. Oh, hello. I wondered if I would hear from you. Tomorrow? Yes, I can make it. Harrow? No, I've never been to that one. Don't worry, I'm sure that I'll find it. Great. See you tomorrow, at noon."

27. Harrow.

I manage to get to the pub just after midday. Although it has only been open less than ten minutes, it is already filling up. It's a large, open-plan pub and I can see that he hasn't arrived yet. I am feeling rather self-conscious, wearing the outfit that I have chosen for this meeting. I don't want him to stick out like a sore thumb, so I have chosen something where his time and 2020 might meet in the middle. I can see that my appearance is attracting the occasional double-take from the market traders of Harrow. Good news: the pub has got a jukebox. I buy a lager and, never being able to resist a jukebox, I browse its selection of music. I am bowled over that in this day and age, it has a collection of Mod classics. I insert my £1 in the slot and immediately, The Four Seasons' 'The Night' fills the main bar. Clutching my beer, I hide behind a pillar, so as not to draw attention to myself.

He arrives and we both notice the first joke of the day. We are dressed identically. He must have had exactly the same thought as me and gone for something that lies midway between the 1850s and the 21st century. As a pair, we look straight out of the chorus of Guys and Dolls. We shake hands and have one of those awkward, not quite a hug, more like a blokey pat on the back, moments. I break the awkwardness:

"It's great to finally meet you. What do you want to drink?"

"I'll have a Cinzano Bianco, please."

"Really? A cinza....."

"Got you there! I think I fancy a large rum."

This is going to be a good crack. I order the rum from the bar and when I get back, he has found a table for two by the taxidermy collection. We toast our meeting, beside a stuffed badger.

"I can't call you great-grandfather. It feels too strange. There are only a few years between us."

I am sixty and he is seventy-six.

"'James' will do nicely."

"This has been a long time coming, James. And I haven't got the first clue what to say."

"You've been on quite an adventure, haven't you? It has been very amusing to watch, as a bystander. For a Neary, you can be dead slow on the uptake."

"You're telling me. Even now, I'm not sure what it has all been about. Do you want to order some food?"

"Not just yet. My sodding gut has been playing me up again this morning."

"Oh, I'm sorry. What's the problem? How are you, really?"

"Dead. Still, dead. Anyway, sod it. I didn't suggest this meet-up so we could talk about our ailments. I'll get us another drink."

As James Neary waits at the bar, I have a good look at him. I have never seen a photo of him and the more that I have learned about him, the more my mental image of him has changed. He looks younger than his age. Most of his hair is still intact. He has a slight stoop, but there is an alertness in his posture that suggests mental strength. His face does not smile in repose, but I have never before seen a pair of eyes so alive. I try to see the signs of the fourteen-year-old powder monkey and I find him in the spirit of the man. I search for any family resemblance, but this one defeats me. Perhaps there is something in the nose, or perhaps I am clutching at straws. Maybe each generation loses something from their resembling family features. I can certainly see something of my Granddad Henry in him; less so, of my Dad. My last selection from the jukebox starts. It's Frank Wilson. Indeed it is. I decide to stop my comparison game. After all, I no longer look like that nervously cocky young herbert from the Railway Tavern. "Snap out of it, Neary. This is not about physical characteristics."

James returns with the drinks. In for a penny, in for a pound:

"You didn't get to meet my Dad, did you?"

"Nope. Fine man, though. One of the quiet ones."

"Have you met him.....since....you know?"

"Nope. Seen him a few times, but we've never talked. It usually works best if the living make the introductions, like you did last night with your other great-grandfathers."

"Wow. I hadn't realised that is how it works. Do you want me to arrange for Dad and you....."

"Nope. That's what I meant about you being slow on the uptake."

"How come?"

"Tell me. How much of this have you contrived? None of it, right?"

"I don't think so. It's just kinda happened. I've tried to not resist anything and go along with it."

"Nothing just happens. We allow something to happen, but we don't manipulate it into happening. You're just a channel for the happening to take place."

"Say more? I think I get it."

"Do you remember that evening when I went on a fishing trip with old Victor? We talked about this shit, all those years ago. We came to the conclusion that to make something happen in your life, it requires love, and belief, and courage. You call it something else, don't you?"

"Balls."

"Yeah, balls. Find someone to love, find something to believe in and find the courage to live life"

"And you reckon that's all there is? That's all this has been about? Those three things have made this adventure happen?"

"Might be. Isn't that enough? Who knows? Only some bugger who is cleverer than me or you."

I look around the pub. I picture Steven and, for some reason, Justice Peter Jackson. His talk about being bold and brave comes to mind. James was, no, is, bold. I don't know for sure, but perhaps he is being very bold today, returning to Harrow for the first time in nearly two centuries. I am reluctant to position myself in the same bold category as James and Jackson. I go to get some more drinks instead. The Mod medley has finished and some joker has replaced it with Kenneth Williams singing, 'Oh, What a Beauty'. James rolls his eyes.

"Do you mind if I ask? What was it like leaving the Navy after all those years and starting over again in civvy street?"

"Tough. And then I met Jane. Got myself a good job. I always felt like I lived two lives. No point in comparing the two either. That only sets up bad feeling."

"I found some old documents. Your father's will. He didn't leave you anything?"

"Why should he? He didn't owe me anything. In his eyes, I rejected all that he stood for. Of course, it wasn't really like that, but that's how he saw it."

"All my four great-grandfathers turned their back on what might have been expected of them. You and the grocer's shop. William Culley left the farm to join the army. Tom Fleetwood became a lighterman instead of working in the tailor's shop. And after several generations of builders, Charlie Worley became a publican. I admire that, more than I can say. That's belief and balls."

"We were lucky. We lived at a time of opportunity that was unheard of for our fathers and their fathers."

"I think you're being too modest. Your brothers stayed on in the shop, but something in you couldn't settle for that."

"Perhaps we were four dreamers? Four stubborn dreamers. What hope is there for you?"

James laughs. He knows that he is playing down his achievements.

"I'm over the moon that I'm from such stock."

"Your mother got it spot on, that night in your flat. Only the living can tell their stories. You have to tell your tale whilst you're living. Have to, with a capital 'H'. That's the time to make your mark, Mark. It's too late, when you're dead. Then it's down to someone else to tell the story."

"Like the man said, the powerful play goes on and you may contribute a verse."

"If you say so, clever arse. I've got a lot of faith in your son. He tells the stories as they ought to be told."

"This may be bollocks, but I'm thinking of calling the book, 'Lines'. What do you think?"

"Bloodlines?"

"Some of it. But there's all sorts of lines, aren't there? I dunno. How about, lines connected by values, for starters? Spiritual lines? Fate lines? And that doesn't even touch on timelines."

"Let's go back to your question from before. What you said about civvy street. There were lines on board the ship in China and there were lines, walking through the park with Jane. I'm no brainbox, but I reckon that they were the same lines. And the daftest thing is, I think they are the same lines that are here, right now."

"Connecting you and me?"

"Partly. Connecting life with life. Connecting history with the future. Connecting what really matters."

I need a piss. At the urinal, the fog in my head starts to feel less foggy. I am starting to get a handle, some traction, on all of this. This isn't a sentimental, nostalgic trip to the past. This is the present tense. These daft suits that James and I are both wearing are the past and the present and the lines between them are what matter the most. I return to the bar.

"Are you getting there, young Mark?"

"Haha. Young Mark! I'm sixty! I spent a lot of time recently thinking about me at fourteen and twenty and at forty, comparing me to you at the same ages. On one level, they were similar lives. Different times with different backdrops, but you were as much of a herbert at twenty as I was, just with more responsibility. More having to grow up quickly...."

"More syphilis."

"That too."

"I can't explain this very well, but I think the times when it seems impossible to compare our lives is the time when our lines are the strongest? What do you reckon?"

"Phew. That's a tricky one. James, look. I'm out of words. This needs sleeping on. We could discuss this until the cows come home, and that would be great, but right at this minute, I just fancy hanging out for a bit."

"That sounds right up my street. Another bevvy?"

"James, would you do me the greatest honour and accompany me to the dogs? I understand that there's a dog track around here somewhere and I hear that you're quite partial to a flutter."

"I couldn't think of anything that I would like to do more. In these suits, we will be a right couple of swells."

We knock back the last of our drinks and step outside into Harrow's blazing August sun.

Only, it is snowing. Huge great flakes practically cover us within seconds of stepping outside. I am not sure that we are even in Harrow. The horses drawing the carriages clip-clop along the street. Street urchins are having a riotous time in the snow. The well-to-do locals are taking shelter in the affluent shops. Outside the pub is a newspaper vendor. The headline on his stand reads: 'LONDON RAILWAY STRIKE NOW IN ITS THIRD DAY'. I take a look around me and know that we have walked out of the pub and smack into 1911, North Kensington. My grandfather, James's son Henry, is probably sitting down on the tracks at Paddington Station, right at this very moment.

I turn to James to point out to him that his son has made the front pages at Fleet Street.

James has collapsed to the floor. He is shivering and struggling for breath. From somewhere deep in my memory bank, something fearful stirs. I shout out to the newspaper seller.

"Hey, mate. What's the date today?"

"Tuesday."

"Not the day. What's the bloody date?"

"Calm down, soppy trousers. Don't you get snipey with me. It's the twenty-eighth of January."

"Shit. And it's 1911, right?"

"Have you been on the sauce, old-timer? Of course it's 1911. It's been 1911, all month."

I take a deep breath; the deepest breath that I can muster. I know something that my great-grandfather doesn't know. Today is the day that James Neary dies.

I struggle to get James home. I have no idea where a hospital is, even if one exists. This is pre-NHS. Do I need to find the neighbourhood's medicine woman with her poultices and leeches? James insists that he wants to be at home. We struggle through the slippery streets of Kensington. Eventually, I find Thorpe Mews and practically have to carry him upstairs to his flat above the stables. I get him into bed, noticing that he is still in his Sky Masterson suit. I am not sure whether he is sleeping or has slipped out of consciousness. Thankfully, the old sea dog is still breathing.

I don't want to leave him, but I need some help. I quickly run outside and plead with a neighbour to fetch a doctor. One of the stable boys offers to go and find Jane. He believes that she is visiting her daughter, on the other side of Kensington.

When I get back to the flat, James is awake.

"This is it, Chick. It's the end, isn't it?"

"I think so. Yes, it's the end."

"One last look at the waves, eh matey? The last story."

I hold my great-grandfather's hand. It is stone cold and soaking with sweat.

"It's never the last story."

"It's okay. I'm at peace with that. I've told my last story. Now it's over to Henry to tell his. And then it will be your father's turn. And then you. To everything there is a season, as the chaplain used to say."

James's breathing becomes more laboured. I can see him leading his men at Port Royal. I can see him driving his master in his coach. I can see his pride in Henry's stand at Paddington. I can see the teenager, suffocated by the shop in Harrow. I can see the lines between him and my son. I couldn't feel prouder in having this man as my great-grandfather.

"Will you stay with me, Mark? Until Jane gets here."

"I'm here, Captain. I ain't going anywhere.

28. Lines.

Wednesday

It is coming to an end. There doesn't feel like too much left to do now. James Hamlet Daubney will be arriving early on Friday morning to collect the camper van for Mr. Vanderbilt. I keep replaying the conversations I had with James Neary, and with all the other ghosts. It feels like the lines are almost complete; or at least as complete as they will ever be.

There are two more journeys that I would like to make. Today, I have got up early to take the train to Dorset. Steven and the support workers are otherwise engaged, so I am flying solo for this one. It is strange that the first line that James mentioned was bloodlines because this trip isn't a bloodline. It feels important, nonetheless. It feels like it shaped something for the generation immediately above me, so subsequently, shaped me. In the middle of a World War, it was a tiny tragedy that received very little attention, but in the vault of family secrets, I believe that it occupied a large space.

I arrive in Portland just before noon. I have only been here before, three times in my life. The last time was nearly twenty-five years ago, but it all feels achingly familiar. I remember the unbounded joy, as an eight-year-old, staying in a sweet shop for a week. That first day of exploring the large flat above the shop and pulling back the heavy maroon drapes in the back sitting room which revealed the stockroom. Boxes and boxes of sweets and chocolates; huge sealed jars of kola cubes and acid drops. I didn't even want to eat them; it was enough to stare at them. To stroke the jars in much the same way that I used to stroke the books in Doctor Pragnell's library.

I am not planning on visiting the sweet shop in Fortuneswell. In 1997, I was desperate to show Steven one of my favourite childhood haunts. We took the bus to Portland Bill, but what I didn't know was that a one-way system had been introduced, so we didn't see the shop until our return journey from the lighthouse. I didn't have a specific picture of the shop stored in my head, but in 1997, it looked like any other municipal newsagent. We stayed on the bus.

I find the market square. Portland is like many coastal towns, perhaps even more so, in that its history is breathing with a fine pair of lungs and the modern, somehow, finds a place to nestle within it. The sweet shop is a perfect microcosm of this. And nothing links the past and the present better than the memorial stone that I am now looking at. A roll- call of one small branch of my family:

Farwell. Archer

Farwell. Charles W

Farwell. Charlotte M.B

Farwell. Diane

Farwell. Nellie

Farwell. Violet.

All six of them, killed on 15th April 1941 when a bomb dropped on their sweet shop. You don't need to know the story to know who is who. You can piece things together by the generational nature of their names. Archer and Nellie were the parents. Their children were: Charles (24), Violet (19) and Charlotte (14). Diane had married one of the other Farwell sons the previous day. He only survived because he just got a twenty-four hour pass from the army and was back at his camp by the time that the bomb fell. Six people whose demise was so sad that it was locked away in the Worley safe, for at least two generations.

I leave some flowers and make a silent apology to Uncle Albert for all those times I dismissed him for being a miserable sod.

Thursday

I woke up this morning feeling even more resistant to today's plan than I have been feeling for the past few days. Only, my gut is telling me that if I don't go through with it, there will be all hell to pay. It all feels rather pointless. I did the trip before, back in 1995, to show Steven the four most important places from my childhood. Three of them had long gone, leaving not a solitary trace that they had even existed. But it feels disrespectful to argue against the will of the universe, so we cancel Steven's water aerobics class and head off to Southall Rec for a picnic. The recreation ground was situated at the bottom of Florence Road. As we lived at number one Florence Road, it was the length of the whole street away. The Rec acted as a short cut to most of my relative's homes. All the

Sunday afternoon visits to relations went via the Rec. For me, the Rec was a second home. Three full-sized football pitches; the tennis courts, the playground with its concrete climbing equipment. They all paled into insignificance though, as from the age of seven and throughout my teenage years, the main attraction of the Rec was the open-air, unheated swimming pool. It occupied an elevated position in the park. You had to climb a dozen steps before you reached the clanging turnstiles. If you looked back, before entering the pool, you caught a marvellous, panoramic view of the whole Rec. Once inside, you were in very much a product of its age. The heavy, metal baskets to keep your clothes in; the changing rooms with the big gaps at the top and bottom of the doors; the constant swooshing sound of the ornamental fountain. Many rites of passage for me happened at Southall swimming pool. My first cigarette, my first snog, my first proper fight. During the long summer holidays of my teenage, there was nowhere in the world that I would rather be.

Today, in its place, is a large, steep, grassy mound. I read somewhere that they never removed the tank, so it is buried deep for archaeologists to discover in many years time. When you look at the mound today, it is impossible to imagine that the pool was even there. The space doesn't look anywhere near big enough. A young couple in their twenties are sitting on the remains whilst absorbed in their smartphones. I am too reverential to sit on that spot, so we set up camp near to where the bowling green used to be. That, also, is now just a wide open space. We tuck into our nosh, whilst I entertain the troops with anecdotes from my formative years.

We are on the last course of cake when it begins. The ground where the pool once stood starts to violently shake. The young couple run down the small hill pretty smartish and settle besides us. It has the appearance of what a minor earthquake might look like, but the grass that we are sitting on is completely stable. As is the rest of the park. The noise starts to become deafening; a crunching, grinding, whirring sound that feels like it could shatter eardrums. A cloud of dust and dirt renders the whole space, practically invisible. But the fall-out is confined. We haven't got a single piece of debris over our Bakewell Tart. A small crowd is beginning to gather. People are covering their ears to shield themselves from the orchestra of nature. We are frozen to our picnic blanket. What should feel like unbearable danger, doesn't, and although we cannot see what is happening, our eyes are glued to the cloudy turbulence.

The thunderous noise continues for about fifteen minutes and then stops abruptly. We still cannot see anything because the dust clouds show no sign of settling. As loud as the noise has just been, we now stand in ghostly silence. Steven breaks the silence:

"We'd better get our trunks."

The cloud miraculously disperses and we are gifted the majestic sight of Southall Swimming Pool in all its glory. It has risen like the Phoenix and stands proudly in its rightful place. Flocks of excited people are running towards the palace of pleasure, with their towels rolled up, under their arms. We quickly pack up the picnic gear and join in with the procession. It's like the Pied Piper has come to Atlantis. As we reach the top of the steps, I turn back, out of habit, for a look at the park. Nothing has changed in the last twenty minutes. The bowling green is still absent. The playground is still inhabited by boringly, sensible equipment. The maypole is nowhere to be seen. I hand over my money and the turnstile clunks open. It is music that is as resonant as Alvin Stardust singing 'Jealous Mind.' We go in to swim.

Friday.

I am on my own in the flat. The camper van was picked up at 7.30 this morning. Uncle Bob's television torment is over. He can rest in peace. Even though our trips around the country and across time are complete, I don't feel melancholy. I feel satisfied. I feel alone again.

I have got the last chapter of my book to write, so as usual, I lay down on the sofa and wait for the advice from the universe. I have never been surrounded by as many people as I have recently, but now I am back to that familiar state of being on my own.

The images start to appear like the pictures at the end of a child's kaleidoscope.

I am back in the front garden at Florence Road, looking blankly at the wreaths at my mother's funeral. My concentration is broken by a cackling laugh. Riding down Florence Road like a carnival queen is Lousia Paget, waving like Royalty to the mourners. She is standing at the stern of the Warspite. When she sees me alone in the garden, she rummages deep in her pocket and throws something in my direction. It is the broach that was given to her by the ship's captain on the occasion of her birth:

"Go well, my little deerio," she shouts. And with that ear-splitting laugh, she sails off towards the Rec.

I am in my seat in the High Court. We are waiting for the arrival of Justice Peter Jackson to deliver his judgement. I am so nervous; I am unable to focus on anything. I glance across to the press box and Mum and Dad signal to me, a big thumbs up. All their brothers and sisters, my aunts and uncles, are sitting behind them with their arms linked. Uncle Frank is holding up a scroll which reads:

"Magna Carta and the Nearys."

Justice Jackson enters his courtroom.

The last image and I see that I am in the epidural room at Hillingdon Hospital. I don't know whether I will still be alive in four hours time. The swing door to the operating theatre opens and I catch a snatch of the four gowned and masked doctors, waiting to get started on me. For a split second, they remove their masks and I smile when I see that they are: William Culley, Charles Worley, Tom Fleetwood and James Neary.

I know that my lines are in good shape.

OPEN AIR SWIMMING BATHS, SOUTHALL

Printed in Great Britain
by Amazon